VOLUME 1

Start a business with ChatGPT: Non-tech beginners guide to making money online using AI

"Become a Prompt Entrepreneur thanks to the best ChatGPT books written by a Human".

Kyle Balmer

Prompt Entrepreneur
@iamkylebalmer

Cover design by: B Street Digital

Disclaimer

FOR EDUCATIONAL AND INFORMATIONAL PURPOSES ONLY

The information contained in this book and the resources available for download through this book are for educational and informational purposes only.

NOT PROFESSIONAL ADVICE

The information contained in this book and the resources available for download through this book is not intended as, and shall not be understood or construed as, professional advice.

EARNINGS DISCLAIMER

There is no guarantee that you will earn any money using the techniques and ideas in these materials. You should not rely on any revenue, sales, or earnings information we present as any kind of promise, guarantee, or expectation of any level of success or earnings. Your results will be determined by a number of factors over which we have no control, such as your financial condition, experiences, skills, level of effort, education, and changes within the market. Running an online business carries risks, and your use of any information contained on this website is at your own risk.

Contents

Introduction

Welcome to the Prompt Playbook series

These are a series of guides designed to help you start business by leveraging AI, specifically ChatGPT.

Each Playbook walks you through a specific business model or business function step-by-step.

Even if you have no experience in that particular topic each guide is setup to give you the knowledge you need along with the exact process to replicate the results for yourself.

We use AI along the way to make tasks simpler and more achievable. We do NOT use AI to replace all our work. You will still need to put in thought, effort and time.

It is actually possible to fully automate the tasks outlined in these guides using AI - however, the end results will be generic and unlikely to succeed.
Instead we use human creativity aligned with AI to build a business.

Is this written by an AI?

Sadly not! Believe me, if I could get away with having an AI write this at a high enough quality I would! I'm naturally lazy which maybe explains my interest in AI.

Instead these guides are written by a flesh human called Kyle Balmer who hails from London.

I've been asked to add a bio here which, as a natural shy person, I hate. But here goes!

- I hold an MBA and have successfully built and sold two companies in my decade plus of entrepreneurship experience. I've also had a load of failures - which is what we learn from.
- I am an Amazon bestselling author and publish a free weekly newsletter that provides solopreneurs with AI tips, business playbooks, and strategies to scale with confidence
- I spent my 20s in the Vietnam, US (NYC, CA and TX) and China. In Vietnam I co-founded the country's first private free-to-air TV station.
- My first online successful online business was in the Chinese language learning niche. I knew it "worked" when I took 2 weeks at a meditation/yoga retreat in Nepal and came out richer than when I had gone in. Despite not working for two weeks. Automated businesses FTW.

Alright enough about me. Back to the more interesting business and AI stuff.

What's in this Volume

This particular volume contains 4 Playbooks.

- Starting a Newsletter Business using AI

- Starting an Affiliate Marketing Blog using AI
- Publishing a Book on Amazon using AI
- Course Creation using AI

Each Playbook is designed independently of the others. Therefore you can choose which business model to work on first.

I have however placed them in order from simplest to most complicated. Therefore if you plan on doing all these models eventually then it makes sense to work through them in order.

Each Playbook is designed to give you a step by step method of achieving the end goal.

Is it the only method? No!

But each is designed to get you started and into the thick of the business as soon as possible over a series of 5 steps.

Generally we follow this pattern:

- The basics of the business model: Business niche definition
- Basic foundational setup: Tech fundamentals
- Build the product: Content creation
- Getting the word out: Marketing
- Generating revenue: Monetisation.

This will flex depending on the needs of the business model featured in the Playbook.

Some of these Playbooks can be deployed extremely quickly - I know one reader who planned, structured, wrote, published and marketed an Amazon eBook in 3 days using the guide!

Work through the Playbooks at your own speed though - just know that at the end of the process you will have a new business asset that can potentially generate income for years to come. It's well worth the work.

This all sounds a bit scary

This might all be new for you. If you've

i) never started a business and
ii) aren't familiar with AI

Then this might all be sounding a little overwhelming right now. I get it.

In truth though right now is the *easiest* time to

i) start a business and
ii) got involved with AI

These books are designed for complete beginners in both business and in AI. We want as many people as possible to be exposed to these new technologies and the opportunities that they bring.

Currently AI is in its early stages. There's a lot of progress each and every day but in reality you just need to get to grip with a handful of tools. Ignore the 2000 new tools each month and instead focus on the one or two you actually need to be productive.

Right now that's ChatGPT.

As someone who works in AI and tries and experiments with 100s of tools believe me: it all comes back to ChatGPT.

ChatGPT is the workhorse of AI right now. And the skills you learn with it will be applicable to any other AI tools you use in the future. That's because of the way we "talk to AI" - more on this later.

Right now it's imperative you get some basic ChatGPT skills and stop being afraid of it. Lots of people are currently hiding their heads in the sand hoping this whole "AI thing" is hype and will disappear. It will not.

AI is like the arrival of electricity or the internet. It's going to affect all aspects of society, outside of high technology and Silicon Valley. It already is.

The good news is that you are early. And by familiarising yourself and beginning to build businesses *now* with these tools you are at a massive advantage.

These Prompt Playbooks are designed to not only help you set up a business but also to help you get to grips with ChatGPT and other AI technologies.

You'll learn both skills at the same time - by applying the AI advice in these guides to an actual business use case.

The 5 Stages of AI Acceptance

If you've never used ChatGPT before we'll get you set up shortly.

First I want to touch on a pattern I've noticed when I work with clients and introduce AI.

It's so common we made a graphic:

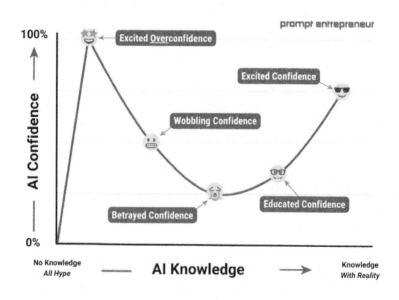

Everyone getting start with AI passes through the following Stages:

Stage 1: Excited Overconfidence

When users first experience ChatGPT, they are overwhelmed by its capabilities. They exclaim, "Wow! This can do anything! I'm never going to have to work again!"

Their excitement fuels an initial burst of overconfidence, as they believe that ChatGPT possesses boundless potential.

Stage 2: Wobbling Confidence

However, as users continue to interact with ChatGPT, they confront its limitations. They may notice that the quality of answers falls short of their expectations, characterised by generic responses and a robotic tone.

This wobbling confidence triggers a moment of doubt. They recognise the potential of ChatGPT but start questioning its real-world usefulness.

Stage 3: Betrayed Confidence

Unfortunately, as users further explore ChatGPT, the situation worsens. They encounter instances where ChatGPT hallucinates or fabricates information.

Additionally, they might confront character limits, misunderstandings, and even the loss of previously discussed conversation elements.

Confidence plummets, and users feel betrayed.

It becomes tempting to dismiss ChatGPT as overhyped and untrustworthy, leading some to abandon it at this early stage.

Stage 4: Educated Confidence

For those who persist through the previous stage, a glimmer of hope emerges. Users begin to grasp that ChatGPT is a tool, one that must be wielded appropriately to yield desired outcomes.

Confidence rekindles as they learn to deploy ChatGPT for the right problems, where its strengths shine. They refine their prompting skills, employing focused, specific, and clear instructions.

With experience, both the quality of their inputs and the resulting outputs improve. This stage is characterized by educated confidence, which derives not from ignorance but from hands-on knowledge.

Stage 5: Excited Confidence

The culmination of this transformative process is Stage 5: excited confidence. Users who reach this stage have mastered the basics and gained a deep understanding of ChatGPT's capabilities and limitations.

They begin to experiment with advanced prompts and explore other AI tools better suited for specific tasks.

Importantly, they recognize that we are still in the early stages of AI development, and ChatGPT's public release in November 2022 represents a mere stepping stone in this technological journey.

Excited confidence stems from a foundation of knowledge and experience, as users eagerly anticipate the future advancements and possibilities that lie ahead.

I've brought this up now to get the jump on any confidence wobbles you have when working with AI. Through working with these Prompt Playbooks I want to take you by the hand and move you from Stage 1 through 5 as quickly as possible.

Once we are at the Stage of Excited Confidence we can actually begin to build businesses. We know how powerful these tools are but we respect their limitations. Importantly we know that any worthwhile endeavour (like building a business!) will still require our time and energy!

It's in this mindset that you'll best profit from the Prompt Playbooks.

Getting set up with ChatGPT

OK enough talk let's get you rolling with ChatGPT.

Nice and simple:

- Head to *https://chat.openai.com/*
- Sign up for a new account

Basic ChatGPT is free. There is a paid alternative which is a better AI model and has other features. If you have the funds I recommend the upgrade. Your results will better than using the free version and the cost is small in the wider scope of setting up a business.

Once logged in you'll see a screen like this:

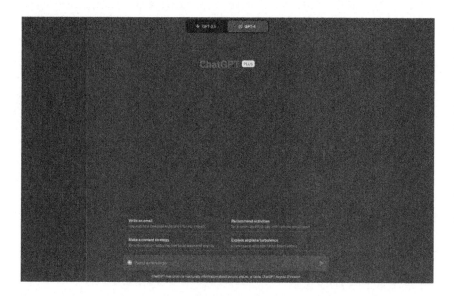

There are two basic elements.

- The Chat area which takes up most of the screen
- The Message area at the bottom of the screen

Go ahead and type "hi" in the message box and then the Send button.

ChatGPT will immediately answer and begin a conversation. Go ahead and chat to ChatGPT.

The "Chat" in the name is a giveaway. That's how we interface with AIs like ChatGPT - just by chatting. In technical terms we're using "natural language" which ChatGPT can understand and respond to.

This is why these modern AIs are such a breakthrough. Normally we'd have to use code to "talk to" a computer. Now we talk to them like we would a human.

All those years of texting and Whatsapp finally pay off!

Let's take ChatGPT for a bit of a ride to see what it can do.
Copy / paste this "prompt" into the message box:

Act as a business analyst

Give me 5 business ideas I can start for under $1000 that leverage AI

For each provide name, description, startup cost breakdown estimate, revenue potential, market size, potential non-generic methods to gain a competitive advantage.

Provide the response in a tabular form

Give me unique rather than generic ideas that can be started by one person and a laptop

Prompt Output:

Absolutely, here's a table of 5 unique AI business ideas that can be launched on a tight budget:

Name	Description	Startup Cost Breakdown	Revenue Potential	Market Size	Competitive Advantage
1. AI Antique Valuer	Uses AI to estimate the value of antiques based on photos and descriptions.	- Software development: $650 - Domain & hosting: $100 - Initial data sets: $150 - Marketing: $100	Fee-based, $10-$50 per valuation.	Antique collectors & sellers.	Specialize in niche categories, collaborate with auction houses.
2. AI Plant Doctor	Diagnoses plant diseases based on images and offers care recommendations.	- Software development: $700 - Domain & hosting: $100 - Initial data sets: $100 - Marketing: $100	Freemium model, with premium advice at $5-$15/query.	Home gardeners, farmers.	Continuous learning from user queries, partnerships with gardening communities.
3. AI Local News Predictor	Predicts local news trends based on social media activity & local events.	- Software development: $650 - Domain & hosting: $100 - Data acquisition: $150 - Marketing: $100	Subscription model, $10-$30 per month.	Local news agencies, bloggers.	Focus on hyper-local regions, real-time updates.
4. AI Recipe Modifier	Adjusts recipes based on dietary needs & available ingredients using AI.	- Software development: $700 - Domain & hosting: $100 - Initial recipe data: $100 - Marketing: $100	Freemium model, with premium features at $5-$20/month.	Home cooks, diet-conscious individuals.	Collaborate with nutritionists, integrate user feedback loops.
5. AI Mood-based Music Composer	Composes music tracks based on user's current mood using AI analysis.	- Software development: $750 - Domain & hosting: $100 - Marketing: $150	Subscription model, $5-$20 per month.	Music enthusiasts, content creators.	Unique mood detection algorithms, partnerships with indie musicians for blending.

Immediately ChatGPT spits out 5 ideas we could set up for under $1000 using AI. Pretty cool.

The **really** powerful stuff however comes when we start to discuss these options with ChatGPT.

We can do this as if we were chatting to a human. If I don't like these ideas and want more I can literally say "give me 5 more".

If I think the startup costs are too high I can say "give me cheaper startup cost options".

If I like a particular idea and want some more variations I can say "option 2, the plant doctor, looks great - can you give me some more variations on that?"

Or if I've decided on one idea I can say "option 2 is perfect. Please flesh out a full business plan, including step by step instructions".

Just play around and test out what ChatGPT can give you. Playing is important - it's how you get used to the interface, capabilities and limitations of ChatGPT.

Prompt Engineering

Prompt Engineering is a much talked about "essential skill" that you may have heard about. Basically prompt engineering is how we "talk to" an AI. It's the way we communicate.

It's useful to think of AI as a hyper-intelligent but not very smart assistant - someone who, when given the right instructions, will excel beyond your wildest imagination. But if they are given bad instructions they won't be able to work out how to do the simplest of tasks.

Prompt engineering is how we structure our requests to AI so that it can do its best work for us.

A great example here is writing a blog article.

Head into ChatGPT and ask it simply to:

Write a blog about digital marketing.

Again Copy / paste the above "prompt" into the ChatGPT message box.

ChatGPT will happily generate the most boring, generic tripe you've ever come across. It's completed its task - writing an article - but the result will be terrible.

Unfortunately lots of users will get a result like this from ChatGPT and decide it is terrible and stop using it!

The problem here though is the user. The instructions given to ChatGPT were bad and therefore the output was bad.

We have a phrase in computing:

Garbage In, Garbage Out. If you put rubbish in don't expect diamonds.

Instead try copy/pasting this prompt:

Act as an SEO copywriter.

Write a blog article opinion piece on the use of AI in digital marketing in healthcare.

Use this structure:
1) Attention Grabbing Headline
2) Intriguing, Short First Sentence
3) Scannable Body Copy
4) Conclusion
5) Call to Action to join newsletter

Output a fully formatted blog article ready to be copied into Wordpress

Use formatting elements like subheaders and bullet points to increase readability.
Work in a formal educational style.
Focus on the keywords "digital marketing" , "healthcare marketing" and "AI in healthcare". Use these organically, focusing on readbility first and foremost.
Generate 750 words

The blog article output from this prompt will be a lot higher quality than the first generic one. Primarily because we've give ChatGPT more to work with.

This is the essence of prompt engineering. It's a communication not a technical skill. If you are good at written communication with humans you'll be good at prompt engineering.

The Perfect Prompt

This isn't a full prompt engineering course but I want to give you my Perfect Prompt framework that you can use in 95% of situations.

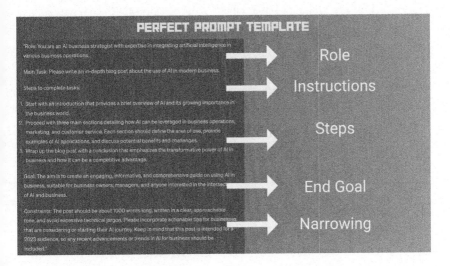

This template uses the RISEN framework:

- **R for Role.** Start each prompt by putting ChatGPT into a role. For example: "Act as a market analyst", "Pretend you're a brand consultant", "Simulate a product manager's perspective". This sets a frame for ChatGPT that allows it it focus on the most relevant information for you.

- **I for Instructions.** Tell ChatGPT what it is you want to do upfront. Clearly specify the main task for ChatGPT to complete.
- **S for Steps**. Break the task down into steps to help guide ChatGPT's process and output. Much in the same way as you wouldn't give a junior employee a task without given some guidance on what the actual steps to complete it are make sure to provide ChatGPT with a breakdown.
- **E for End Goal**. Specify what success looks like to you. How else will ChatGPT know what to aim for? If you want the results in a table then say so - don't assume ChatGPT can read your mind.
- **N for Narrowing**. Provide constraints to finesse the output. Want a certain tone of voice, a minimum/maximum word count, a different language? Add these details to finalise the output.

If you apply this framework to your prompts you'll automatically be ahead of 95% of ChatGPT users out there. So write it on a stickie note for easy reminders.

All the prompts in the Playbooks will be pre-written for you using this format **but** it's handy for you to know for when you need to go off piste and work with ChatGPT independently. Which I fully encourage!

Time to jump in

That's enough theory and preamble. Now's the time to get stuck in and start building. This is a very hands on book so you can't get away with just reading I'm afraid!

Now it's time for you to choose which Playbook to get started on and get going. Maybe scan through the introductions to each of them and see which takes you fancy.

All of them will equip you with essential AI skills for the future as well as, if implemented, a revenue generating asset.

If still uncertain about which to start with I'd recommend going with the the first Playbook on starting a Newsletter business. This can help you with *any* other business you want to start and so is a strong foundation to start with.

Start an Email Newsletter Business with AI

What is a newsletter business?

Newsletters are curated email publications that provide subscribers with regular updates, insights, and valuable content on specific topics of interest. Importantly newsletters are NOT the email marketing you get from companies that you interact with.

You know the type - you buy some nails at Home Depot and they send you emails for years about their Thanksgiving offers.

We're NOT talking about that. Those are company newsletters that a marketing a business.

Instead we're talking about newsletters that ARE the business. The business is in writing, publishing and growing and audience. And then monetising that audience. It's a subtle but important difference.

Some successful examples of newsletters run as businesses include Morning Brew, a daily business newsletter that provides concise and engaging summaries of the latest news and trends in the business world. Morning Brew sold for $75m.

Another example is Milk Road, a newsletter that focuses on web3 and crypto and was sold for 8 figures just 10 months after starting.

Both of these newsletters have managed to attract a large and dedicated subscriber base by consistently delivering high-quality content that meets the needs and interests of their target audience.

Why is the newsletter business exciting?

They have gained significant popularity in recent years due to their ability to deliver personalized and relevant information directly to subscribers' inboxes.

This is a huge deal for advertisers recently because Meta/Google advertising rates are increasing whilst tracking of results (because of privacy laws and things like the iOS 14 update) is becoming harder and harder.

Entering the newsletter business as a writer is exciting right now because it offers significant financial opportunities.

Newsletters can generate income through various channels such as paid subs, sponsorship, affiliate marketing, and advertising.

One newer revenue source recommending other newsletters. You know that the people reading your newsletter like newsletters. And you know what subjects you like. So by simply recommending other newsletters you can make ~$1-2/referred subscriber. Pretty cool!

Additionally, as newsletters allow for direct communication with subscribers, writers can build a loyal and engaged audience, which can further enhance their earning potential through partnerships, collaborations, and even book deals.

Once you have an audience the sky is really the limit.

The potential for financial success in the newsletter business is high, making it an enticing venture for writers.

OK what about AI?

Newsletters have been around for years but they are *particularly* exciting right now because of the advances in AI that we've seen this year.

AI is particularly valuable for
- curating content from your topic
- idea generation
- newsletter outlines
- drafting your newsletter
- editing and correcting your newsletter
- social media to promote your articles
- and more

You *could* set up an AI to automatically generate a whole newsletter. It would basically find other quality sources in your subject area and rewrite/ compile them into a newsletter.

That's not what we're going to focus on, even if it sounds very appealing.

Why not?

It's not a sustainable business model.

If it's that easy lots of other entrepreneurs will enter the market and do *exactly* the same thing.

Supply will rise, demand will stay the same.

The value of the pure AI generated newsletters will fall to zero.

Instead we're going to utilise AI alongside our own creativity to make something unique enough to stand out whilst still not being a full time job.

Capiche?

Structure of the guide

These guides are no-holds-barred, full walkthroughs of the steps you need to take.

Setting up a new business and adding an income steam is not easy. It's not meant to be easy.

But you follow along and ACT (rather than just read) and you'll have the basic foundations of a newsletter business in place.

In brief here's what's in this playbook:

- **Part 1:** Understanding Newsletters
- **Part 2:** Setting up your newsletter
- **Part 3:** Content Creation with AI - Part 1
- **Part 4:** Content Creation with AI - Part 2 & Audience Building
- **Part 5:** Monetization: Advertising and Sponsorships

I've intentionally split this guide up over five emails so you have a handful of actions to do daily.

At the end of the process this will be compiled into a (short) book.

Connect with me on Twitter (@iamkylebalmer) and let me know how it's going.

Understanding Newsletters and Niche Selection

We've covered a lot of "theory" above so today's actions are more limited.

1. Identify Your Interests and Skills

We're going to borrow and adapt a prompt we've used before :

> As a brainstorming assistant, generate a list of 50 potential newsletter niches based on my interests in [insert interests here] combined with my skills [insert skills here]
>
> The goal is to come up with unique and engaging content niche that combine these interests and skills.
>
> Combine where they naturally intersect but do not force combinations. Please avoid overly wide niches.

Sit down with a pen and paper (I know, medieval!) and sketch out your interests and skills.

Why paper? It's easier to avoid self editing.

Just go nuts and get as much down on paper as possible. We'll let ChatGPT do the sorting.

If something falls under interest and skills add it to both. This is normal. What we are interested in we tend to do more. And doing it more makes us skilled at it.

Prompt Output

In this example I inputted

[interests] = AI, productivity, writing, board games, video games, weightlifting, cycling, entrepreneurship
[skills] = systems thinking, writing, AI, endurance sports, entrepreneurship, business strategy

Add more if you can, the more the better.

 1. "AI & Productivity: Streamlining Your Life with Technology"
2. "Writing for AI: How to Craft Content for Machine Learning"
3. "Board Game Strategies: System Thinking for Game Night"
4. "Video Games AI: How AI Shapes Your Gaming Experience"
5. "Weightlifting Algorithms: Applying AI to Your Fitness Routine"
6. "Cycling Endurance: Boosting Performance through Systems Thinking"
7. "AI Entrepreneurship: Disrupting Industries with Innovative Technology"
8. "Interactive Storytelling: Writing for Video Games"
9. "Cycling Business: Strategies for Sports Entrepreneurship"
10. "Strength in Systems: Applying Systems Thinking to Weightlifting"
11. "Entrepreneur's Board: Strategic Decision-Making Lessons from Board Games"
12. "Video Game Startups: Bridging Entrepreneurship and Gaming"
13. "The AI Writer: Exploring AI's Role in Content Creation"
14. "CycleTech: The Intersection of Cycling and Technology"
15. "Game Mechanics: System Thinking in Board and Video Games"
16. "Fitness and Business: Lessons from the Weight Room to the Board Room"
17. "AI in Endurance Sports: Enhancing Performance with Technology"
18. "The Art of Productivity in Video Game Development"
19. "From Game Board to Board Room: Entrepreneurship Lessons"
20. "Cycling & AI: Revolutionizing Biking with Technology"

These are the first 20 of 50.

Keep generating and copy/paste the ones that you like.

When you have ~10 ideas that sound good to you (based on your interests and skills) feed them back into ChatGPT and tell it that these are your favourites and to generate more ideas based of those.

2. Identify money niches

Combining interests and skills is a first step.

But this is a business. We need to make sure that the newsletter we create can also generate an income.

Therefore we need a third variable: a good market!

Here's the next prompt:

> As a marketing strategist analyse this list of newsletter business ideas. This business involves creating a newsletter, building an audience and then monetising the audience through advertising and sponsorships.
>
> Analyse them by these factors: total market size(+), value of subscribers(+) and competition(-). Score each factor out of 100 and use this to create a composite total score of 300 for the attractiveness of the newsletter business idea.
>
> Sort all entries by their composite score, highest composite score at the top then descending. Present results in tabular form.

Prompt Output

Here's my ranking using ideas from the previous step.

Newsletter Business Idea	Market Size Score (+)	Subscriber Value Score (+)	Competition Score (-)	Composite Score
AI Driven Entrepreneurship: Future-Proofing Your Business	85	85	60	210
Video Game Startups: Bridging Entrepreneurship and Gaming	85	80	65	200
Strategic Gaming: Entrepreneurial Lessons from Video Games	80	75	70	185
AI & Productivity: Streamlining Your Life with Technology	75	80	60	195
AI Entrepreneurship: Disrupting Industries with Innovative Technology	80	80	75	185
Video Games AI: How AI Shapes Your Gaming Experience	85	70	80	175
Writing for the Gaming Industry: A Novice's Guide	80	75	85	170
Systems Thinking in Video Game Design	75	75	80	170
Cycling & AI: Revolutionizing Biking with Technology	70	75	75	170
Productivity in Gaming: Efficient Strategies for Gamers	75	70	80	165
AI in Endurance Sports: Enhancing Performance with Technology	65	75	70	170
Weightlifting Algorithms: Applying AI to Your Fitness Routine	60	75	65	170
The AI Gym: How AI is Transforming Fitness	70	70	75	165

Use this ranking to start to filter out ideas that have no obvious market. Lots of mine have solid market potential but this is a function of the interests and skills I put in.

Generally though the big three markets will be the winners here:
- Money
- Health
- Relationships

If you can nail something into one of these big three you're generally going in the right direction.

3. Research other newsletters

Once you've honed in on your rough niche we want to see what the current newsletter landscape is like.

Don't worry about having totally nailed the niche yet. Honestly, it's going to shift and adapt as you get going and work out what your readers want.

You just need to know the topic.

Here's the prompt:

> *Give me a list of newsletters that cover the topic of [copy/paste whole title, description]*

Copy in the whole name and description that ChatGPT generated. For instance "AI Driven Entrepreneurship: Future-Proofing Your Business"

This will give ChatGPT as much context as possible.

Prompt Output

Using the prompt "Give me a list of newsletters that cover the topic of AI Driven Entrepreneurship: Future-Proofing Your Business"

1. **MIT Technology Review's The Algorithm**: It provides thought-provoking articles on the impact of AI on our lives and businesses.
2. **The Artificial Intelligence Times**: It's a daily digest of the most important AI news and updates.
3. **AI Weekly**: This is a weekly collection of the best news and resources on AI and machine learning.
4. **Entrepreneur's newsletters**: Entrepreneur magazine offers a variety of newsletters that often cover the intersection of AI and entrepreneurship.
5. **The Hustle**: It's a daily newsletter covering tech and business news. They sometimes delve into AI and how it influences entrepreneurial ventures.
6. **CB Insights**: It's a tech market intelligence platform that often discusses the role of AI in entrepreneurship.
7. **VentureBeat**: VentureBeat covers a range of tech topics and has a keen focus on AI and machine learning.
8. **Emerj**: Formerly known as TechEmergence, this newsletter provides regular updates on AI trends, particularly as they pertain to businesses and entrepreneurs.
9. **Andreessen Horowitz's Newsletters**: A16z's newsletters often touch on the intersection of AI and business, including entrepreneurship.
10. **Benedict Evans Newsletter**: A well-known industry analyst who often discusses AI in his newsletters.

Warning: this is a case when ChatGPT's learning period comes into play. This is a decent list *but* AI (which is the topic entered into ChatGPT) has exploded since September 2021, the end of ChatGPT's training period.

If you have access to Claude2: *https://claude.ai/* (currently UK and US only) use this tool instead because it's training period is up to 2023. It's free.

Here's Claude2's output:

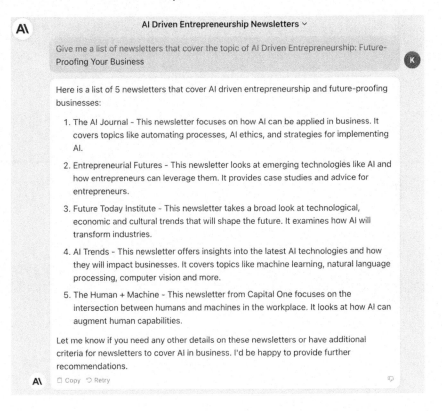

If that's not an option head to _https://_
inboxreads.co/ as a good place to run research.

Once you've got the newsletters go ahead and
subscribe to them all! You need to see what they
are writing about.

We'll be referring to their content in future parts of
this guide.

4. Absorb Matt McGarry's wisdom

Not an AI prompt but potentially the most important action today.

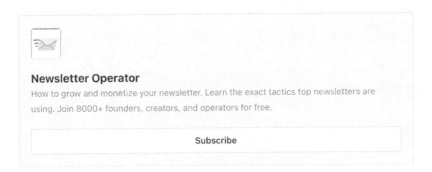

Subscribe to his newsletter.: _https://www.newsletteroperator.com/_

Why? It's run by Matt McGarry who is THE newsletter guy. He talks about how to grow and monetise a newsletter and is basically the best in the biz.

If you are serious about making a profitable newsletter business his emails are gold-dust - it's all actionable and tested advice.

Pulling it together

That's everything for this part.

It's been a theory heavy part rather because I needed to outline what exactly a newsletter business is and what we're going to be working towards over the next week.

There will be more actions in the next 4 steps, don't worry!

Setting up your newsletter

The previous part was very theory heavy so you understood what sort of business we're working on this week.

Now will be very action heavy to get the basics in place.

Also, only some of these will use AI today. Don't worry - the next two parts when we look at content it'll be 100% prompts!

Without further ado let's crack on.

1. Setting up your Newsletter software

There are a multitude of options for you newsletter tool.

I've used SO many of them over the years. And more recently surveyed them all for one of my other businesses (_emailsponsorship.com_).

I'll cut to the chase: right now beehiiv is the best tool on the market.

It's also free up to 2,500 subscribers which is more than enough for you to start generating an income. Unlike other platforms it also comes with a bunch of built in monetisation tools so you can immediately begin to generate revenue.

I'll go into these in more detail later in Part 5 when we talk about how to generate revenue from your newsletter.

Finally, beehiiv has also embraced AI writing and image creation and built them directly into their tools. As of the time of writing no-one else has.

This suggests beehiiv will be the most friendly with AI creators, which is good news with us.

First step then: grab a free beehiiv account. It's free up until 2,500 subscribers and then reasonable costs for building a business.

If you want to support me then here's a link that means I get paid if/when you get a paid plan: **Sign up to beehiiv:** *https://tinyurl.com/53sszm6d* (affiliate). No extra cost to you.

If you think I'm stinky and your spite reading this newsletter then here's the non-affiliate link: Sign up to beehiiv: *https://www.beehiiv.com/* (non-affiliate).

Use either - I won't be (too) mad!

How do you know I actually think beehiiv is good?

I publish my Prompt Entrepreneur newsletter daily using beehiiv - it's what I personally use!

2. Test AI writing tool

Next up we're going to test out beehiiv's AI writing tool. Tomorrow we'll get into depth with the actual content - for now I want you to see the ease with which we can generate quality content.

If you aren't using beehiiv this will also work in ChatGPT. You'll just need to copy/paste into your newsletter platform of choice.

If in beehiiv create a draft of a newsletter. Don't worry, we'll delete it. Once in the draft just type /ai to bring up the AI writer or tap the plus symbol then select AI Writer.

You'll see something like this:

In settings you can tell it how many paragraphs to create and set the language and the tone of voice.

Here's how to play around and experiment with the tool:

- Start by choosing a specific topic or question you want the AI to write about.

- Use clear and concise instructions to guide the AI in the desired direction.
- Experiment with different writing styles, tones, or perspectives to see how the AI adapts.
- Play around with the length of the input prompt to see how it affects the output.
- Try asking the AI to generate a story, poem, or even a joke for some fun and creative results.
- Experiment with different genres or themes to see how the AI can generate content tailored to specific needs.
- Use the AI as a brainstorming tool by asking it to generate ideas or provide insights on a particular subject.
- Explore the AI's capabilities by asking it to write in different languages or imitate famous authors.
- Collaborate with the AI by providing partial sentences and letting it complete them, creating a unique blend of human-AI writing.

Useful list? Great: beehiiv's AI generated all of that. I hardly lifted a finger.

Also, this same tool can be used to rewrite content that you write yourself - to make it shorter, longer, simpler etc. It's a very powerful tool.

For now just test it out. We'll be going into depth in Parts 3 and 4.

3. Deciding your newsletter format

The last two steps have hopefully shown you how much time can be saved compiling a newsletter using AI.

A huge barrier for most people is the time it'll take to write a newsletter and create or find images for it. These barriers are now much lower.

We're going to go into a LOT more detail about newsletter content creation over the next 2 days.

All I want right now is for the time/energy barrier to have been surmounted so that you can think freely about what sort of newsletter you can now create. We have 3 choices to make.

Choice 1 : Source of content

There are two basic types of newsletter:

- Content creation
- Content curation

Content creation newsletters are based on you creating content from scratch. These tend to be newsletters that inform, educate or entertain based on your personal skills and take on life.

This newsletter that you are reading is creation focused: every day I'm sitting down to write this out

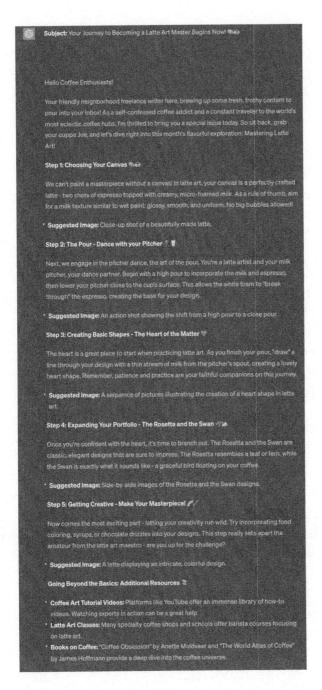

Subject: Your Journey to Becoming a Latte Art Master Begins Now! ☕️

Hello Coffee Enthusiasts!

Your friendly neighborhood freelance writer here, brewing up some fresh, frothy content to pour into your inbox! As a self-confessed coffee addict and a constant traveler to the world's most eclectic coffee hubs, I'm thrilled to bring you a special issue today. So sit back, grab your cuppa Joe, and let's dive right into this month's flavorful exploration: Mastering Latte Art!

Step 1: Choosing Your Canvas ☕️

We can't paint a masterpiece without a canvas! In latte art, your canvas is a perfectly crafted latte - two shots of espresso topped with creamy, micro-foamed milk. As a rule of thumb, aim for a milk texture similar to wet paint: glossy, smooth, and uniform. No big bubbles allowed!

* **Suggested Image:** Close-up shot of a beautifully made latte.

Step 2: The Pour - Dance with your Pitcher ☕️🥛

Next, we engage in the pitcher dance, the art of the pour. You're a latte artist and your milk pitcher, your dance partner. Begin with a high pour to incorporate the milk and espresso, then lower your pitcher close to the cup's surface. This allows the white foam to "break through" the espresso, creating the base for your design.

* **Suggested Image:** An action shot showing the shift from a high pour to a close pour.

Step 3: Creating Basic Shapes - The Heart of the Matter ♥️

The heart is a great place to start when practicing latte art. As you finish your pour, "draw" a line through your design with a thin stream of milk from the pitcher's spout, creating a lovely heart shape. Remember, patience and practice are your faithful companions on this journey.

* **Suggested Image:** A sequence of pictures illustrating the creation of a heart shape in latte art.

Step 4: Expanding Your Portfolio - The Rosetta and the Swan 🌿🦢

Once you're confident with the heart, it's time to branch out. The Rosetta and the Swan are classic, elegant designs that are sure to impress. The Rosetta resembles a leaf or fern, while the Swan is exactly what it sounds like - a graceful bird floating on your coffee.

* **Suggested Image:** Side-by-side images of the Rosetta and the Swan designs.

Step 5: Getting Creative - Make Your Masterpiece! 🎨🖌️

Now comes the most exciting part - letting your creativity run wild. Try incorporating food coloring, syrups, or chocolate drizzles into your designs. This step really sets apart the amateur from the latte art maestro - are you up for the challenge?

* **Suggested Image:** A latte displaying an intricate, colorful design.

Going Beyond the Basics: Additional Resources 📚

* **Coffee Art Tutorial Videos:** Platforms like YouTube offer an immense library of how-to videos. Watching experts in action can be a great help.
* **Latte Art Classes:** Many specialty coffee shops and schools offer barista courses focusing on latte art.
* **Books on Coffee:** "Coffee Obsession" by Anette Moldvaer and "The World Atlas of Coffee" by James Hoffmann provide a deep dive into the coffee universe.

from scratch. Actually, I'm standing at a standing desk but that's not important!

Content curation newsletters on the other hand are about finding existing content that someone else had made and bringing it together in a single newsletter.

Curation could be:
- a single link (ie For the Interested: _https://fortheinterested.com/_)
- multiple links (ie. Javascript Weekly: _https://javascriptweekly.com/issues/647_)

Whatever their particular format what they have in common is that they are based off existing content rather than on new content.

Our recommendation is to create a newsletter that is a bit of content creation and a bit of content curation.

Stacked Marketer: _https://www.stackedmarketer.com/full-newsletters/public-content/_ is a great example of this. The core content is curation - it's a set of interesting news stories, product launches and educational links. But the publisher also adds a few paragraphs of context about why these links are useful.

This is a strong combination of curation (the links) and creation (the editorial comment).

The rest of this guide will work whether you are creating or curating. But we'll use a mixed hybrid of creation/curation moving forward.

For now your action is to simply to decide the format - creation or curation.

Choice 2: Volume of content

Next up - what's the length of your content?

Going back to For the Interested you'll see that this email is literally one line of context and one link.

This newsletter has over 40k subscribers and charges $350 to sponsor an issue. It's published daily so that's ~$127,750 per annum for one sentence a day.

So: short can work!

Alternatively there are newsletters like this one which are much more long form. It's a creation based newsletter than matches my style of creation - in-depth guides.

In the middle there are newsletters like Stacked Marketer than have 5 or so items per issue. 5 links, with 5 pieces of context.

Your choice will depend on what is most valuable for your niche. And that's based on your own expertise in this area as well as your research you did when subscribing to competitor newsletters.

What do you think will be most valuable? Indeed, as someone who is interested in this topic: what length of newsletter would you want to read?

Choice 3: Publishing schedule

The third choice is *how* often you'll publish.

For the Interested, Stacked Marketer and this newsletter are daily.

Other newsletters are weekly. Some are even monthly.

I'd recommend minimum once a week. Daily if you have the time and inclination.

Why? More issues means more sponsor slots which will be important when we come to monetise the newsletter.

How often you publish will really depend on what priority this business is to you. If you are uncertain start with weekly. And then if it takes off look at moving to 3x/week or even daily.

4. Newsletter description

Now we're going to generate some assets to plug into our new beehiiv to start making our newsletter more professional.

First up the newsletter description. Here's the prompt:

> *Act as a marketing copywriter. I have a new newsletter about [topic] the content is primarily [original content/content curation/ mix of original content and content curation]*
>
> *The newsletter is published every [time period]*
>
> *It is a [long/short] newsletter - focus on the benefits of its length*
>
> *Give me 10 potential titles for this newsletter as well as a short description of the newsletter*

Prompt Output

Using the prompt :

Act as a marketing copywriter. I have a new newsletter about Driven Entrepreneurship: Future-Proofing Your Business

The content is primarily mix of original content and content curation The newsletter is published every week It is a short newsletter - focus on the benefits of its length

Give me 10 potential titles for this newsletter as well as a short description of the newsletter.

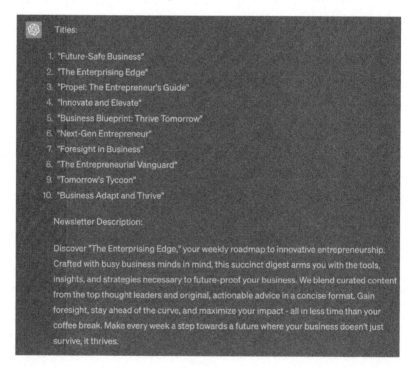

Titles:

1. "Future-Safe Business"
2. "The Enterprising Edge"
3. "Propel: The Entrepreneur's Guide"
4. "Innovate and Elevate"
5. "Business Blueprint: Thrive Tomorrow"
6. "Next-Gen Entrepreneur"
7. "Foresight in Business"
8. "The Entrepreneurial Vanguard"
9. "Tomorrow's Tycoon"
10. "Business Adapt and Thrive"

Newsletter Description:

Discover "The Enterprising Edge," your weekly roadmap to innovative entrepreneurship. Crafted with busy business minds in mind, this succinct digest arms you with the tools, insights, and strategies necessary to future-proof your business. We blend curated content from the top thought leaders and original, actionable advice in a concise format. Gain foresight, stay ahead of the curve, and maximize your impact - all in less time than your coffee break. Make every week a step towards a future where your business doesn't just survive, it thrives.

This is a nice simple prompt that will give you more detail on each of the lessons that ChatGPT has added into the structure.

Again, go through and manually tweak, asking ChatGPT to add/delete or edit as required.

The more we do now with our structure the better our results in tomorrow's Part 3 where we start to generate content.

Pulling it together

Great. By working through today's steps you have the basics of your newsletter in place.

That's the actual platform (beehiiv) but also the foundations of what your newsletter will be actually publishing in each issue.

Continue to review your competitors in the space as you'll keep finding new ideas that you can potentially fold into your newsletter.

This will become important as we move into actually creating content next.

Using AI for newsletter content

In this part we're getting into the meat of our newsletter: the content.

I'm going to cover both content curation and content creation.

We talked about both of these in the last Part so if you have no idea what I'm talking about go back and refresh yourself.

We're going to be quite high level in this issue, giving you the basic prompts for content that you need to get started.

Next we'll look at refinements. Right now just push ahead with making something.

That said...

1. Curation feeds

We're starting with curation because:

i) it's simpler and

ii) even if you are writing original content it's good to keep your finger on the pulse with your topic

This first prompt does both. We're going to find out the exact people and publications we need to be following so that we can either curate from them or simply for original content creation.

Here's our first prompt:

> Act as an online research assistant
>
> I am writing a newsletter about [topic]
>
> Help me research other sources of information in this space Give me 10 blogs, 10 news sites, 10 newsletters, 10 reddit subreddits, 10 twitter influencers, 10 instagram influencers, 10 tiktok influencers,
>
> Present the information in a table.

Prompt Output

For topic = " building side hustles"

And reduced to 2 per category for brevity.

Platform	Handle/Name	Description
Blogs	Side Hustle School	Blog by Chris Guillebeau, author of 'Side Hustle: From Idea to Income in 27 Days'
Blogs	Smart Passive Income	Pat Flynn's blog with insights on running an online business and optimizing it for passive income
News Sites	Entrepreneur.com (side hustle section)	Contains articles about entrepreneurship, including side hustles
News Sites	Business Insider (Small Business section)	Features stories about successful small businesses and side hustles
Newsletters	The Hustle	Daily email newsletter covering updates in business, technology, and startups, with occasional articles on side hustles
Newsletters	Side Hustle School	Daily email newsletter with actionable tips and case studies about side hustles
Reddit Subreddits	/r/sidehustle	A community sharing and discussing side hustle opportunities
Reddit Subreddits	/r/Entrepreneur	A community for both established and aspiring entrepreneurs to discuss business ventures, including side hustles
Twitter Influencers	@chrisguillebeau	Author of 'Side Hustle: From Idea to Income in 27 Days'
Twitter Influencers	@PatFlynn	Known for his work in passive income and online businesses
Instagram Influencers	@chrisguillebeau	Shares tips and tricks for side hustles
Instagram Influencers	@patflynn	Shares strategies for online businesses
TikTok Influencers	@garyvee	Shares tips and motivation for entrepreneurs
TikTok Influencers	@sidehustlepro	Shares strategies for starting side hustles

Note: ChatGPT won't be able to give you the most up to date influencers and blogs because of its training limit.

Therefore supplement this with Google searches - ie "blogs similar to Smart Passive Income" to find more.

Alternatively use a more up to date model like Claude2 if you have access.

In either case you want to pull together a list of 20+ sources that you'll be curating from.

To keep on track of all these sources I recommend an app called Feedly. It can pull together blogs, newsletters, Reddit communities all in one place so you can monitor without having to go to separate parts of the internet.

2. Curation rewriting

Act as a newsletter writer and editor

I will provide you with the text of a post

Convert the post into a short newsletter section

Focus on the main points, removing extraneous details. Condense to 200 words maximum.

Provide a section title

Start with a hook like a question or bold statement. Make each sentence want the reader to move to the next sentence.

Ignore quotes.

Use bullet points when possible

No long paragraphs - use single sentence paragraphs.

Use a [tone] tone of voice.

##Post begins##
[Copy/paste post here]
##Post ends##

This prompt will take an existing article and rewrite it in a format more suitable for a newsletter.

Simply copy/paste the source article you want to use into the prompt at the bottom.

I've also added a tone of voice parameter you can use to modify the output. Try serious, professional, cheeky, funny, rude etc. Or a combination!

One tip here is to take a sample of your own writing, paste it into ChatGPT and ask "How would you describe the tone of voice in this article?"

Here's how ChatGPT describes my writing:

 The tone of voice in this post can be described as:

1. Informative: The author provides a detailed exploration of the various stages of acceptance when using ChatGPT, offering a wealth of information about the user experience.

2. Encouraging: Throughout the post, the author encourages readers to persist, adapt, and learn from their experiences with the AI tool, providing motivation and support.

3. Conversational: The author uses an informal, friendly style, often addressing the readers directly ("Hey Prompt Entrepreneur", "Where are you?") and sharing personal experiences, making it feel like a chat between friends.

4. Insightful: The author exhibits a deep understanding of the user journey with ChatGPT, offering insights into the challenges and rewards of the process.

5. Enthusiastic: The author displays a positive and energetic tone, evident in their excitement about the potential of ChatGPT and the AI community.

So if I wanted to match my tone of voice I'd add "informative, encouraging, conversational, insightful, enthusiastic" tone of voice.

The output will be a short, rewritten version of the original article that you can use in your newsletter.

I'd recommend leaving a Read More link to the original piece - remember you are curating here!

Prompt Output

Based on original article from BBC News - *https://www.bbc.co.uk/news/newsbeat-66174723*

 ###Section Title: The AI Invasion: Dance Music's New Frontline

Are your dance floor moves being orchestrated by artificial intelligence (AI)?

You might be grooving to the rhythm, the beats flowing seamlessly, but the DJ's booth is empty. As technology and financial constraints reshape the music industry, the idea of an AI-manned DJ booth isn't far-fetched. Yet, the human connection - that shared sweat-dripping, heart-thumping experience - could be what keeps AI at bay, insists DJ Nooriyah, a seasoned player on the global circuit.

* AI software is already suggesting mixes based on tempos. But Nooriyah believes that the emotional connection between a DJ and their audience is tough for AI to emulate.
* On the flip side, novice DJ Hannah Rose fears the surge of AI could spell a bleak future for human DJs. Virtual sets and streamed shows are becoming the new norm, driven by cost-saving measures.
* Even when an East London club hosted an AI rave, the crowd found the music "dry and empty." Does this indicate a craving for the human touch?

Yet, the battle is murkier in the production realm. Nooriyah, a music producer herself, acknowledges that AI is already infiltrating the mixing and mastering stages of music production.

* She calls for an urgent dialogue between music insiders and AI developers, suggesting taxation on AI companies to fund training for displaced human artists.

The future of AI in music is in our hands. Will we let it play the tune, or will we continue to champion the human creators behind the melody?

The output will be a short, rewritten version of the original article that you can use in your newsletter.

I'd recommend leaving a Read More link to the original piece - remember you are curating here!

3. Curation editorial

This is a variation of the above prompt for a much shorter editorial comment.

You'll see this sort of curation in a short form newsletter than gives links and maybe a sentence of context per link.

Act as a newsletter writer and editor

I will provide you with the text of a post

Create a short descriptive one sentence hook that makes people want to clock through to read the full post.

##Post begins##
[Copy/paste post here]
##Post ends##

Prompt Output

Which leads to this version with metaphor added:

 "Dive into the pulsating world of dance music and discover how AI threatens to remix the DJ scene – will the beat stay human, or is a silicon takeover imminent?"

Alternatively ask for a super short version by specifying "short descriptive 10 word hook"

 "AI invades dance music: Is the DJ's touch irreplaceable?"

Match length to your newsletter format decided in the previous Part. And if in doubt remember to go and check other newsletters for inspiration.

4. Creation ideation

The last three prompts have been curation focused and give you a solid way to find, condense and editorialise existing content.

Now we're switching to content that we write ourselves.

If you are only doing curation no problem - you can skip these last two prompts and we'll see you in the next part. Early end to school!

If you are creating here's our first prompt:

Act as a newsletter writer and editor

I write a newsletter on [topic]

Provide me with a list of 50 potential newsletter issues I can write, along with the subject line.

Give me a mix of inspirational, instructional, listicle, review, interview, case study, deep dive, personal story, round up, opinion/ editorial, survey, behind the scenes. Provide this information next to the result.

Results in a table.

Prompt Output

Using [topic] = "how to make money using AI tools"

Subject Line	Category
1. "Master AI Tools: Top 10 Picks of the Year"	Listicle
2. "AI Millionaires: Success Stories to Inspire You"	Inspirational
3. "Harness the Power of AI for Profit: A Complete Guide"	Instructional
4. "Revealing the AI Secret Behind My First $10k"	Personal Story
5. "Review: How the Latest AI Software Stacks Up"	Review
6. "Inside Look: How AI Powers Profitable Trading Algorithms"	Behind the Scenes
7. "Your Voice Matters: AI User Experience Survey Results"	Survey
8. "Interview: AI Guru Shares Secrets to Success"	Interview
9. "Profitable Patterns: Case Study on Successful AI Implementations"	Case Study
10. "Editor's Corner: The Future of Making Money with AI"	Opinion/Editorial

This should start giving you a whole lot of ideas for issues. As always, pick out the ones you like and ignore the rest. Then ask for more from ChatGPT, cherrypick the best, repeat.

Continue this until you have 10-20 potential issues to get started with.

Bonus: try adding the line "Do not provide generic suggestions" to get more creative suggestions.

Hello Coffee Enthusiasts!

Your friendly neighborhood freelance writer here, brewing up some fresh, frothy content to pour into your inbox! As a self-confessed coffee addict and a constant traveler to the world's most eclectic coffee hubs, I'm thrilled to bring you a special issue today. So sit back, grab your cuppa Joe, and let's dive right into this month's flavorful exploration: Mastering Latte Art!

Step 1: Choosing Your Canvas ☕

We can't paint a masterpiece without a canvas! In latte art, your canvas is a perfectly crafted latte - two shots of espresso topped with creamy, micro-foamed milk. As a rule of thumb, aim for a milk texture similar to wet paint: glossy, smooth, and uniform. No big bubbles allowed!

* **Suggested Image:** Close-up shot of a beautifully made latte.

Step 2: The Pour - Dance with your Pitcher ☕ 🥛

Next, we engage in the pitcher dance, the art of the pour. You're a latte artist and your milk pitcher, your dance partner. Begin with a high pour to incorporate the milk and espresso, then lower your pitcher close to the cup's surface. This allows the white foam to "break through" the espresso, creating the base for your design.

* **Suggested Image:** An action shot showing the shift from a high pour to a close pour.

Step 3: Creating Basic Shapes - The Heart of the Matter ♥

The heart is a great place to start when practicing latte art. As you finish your pour, "draw" a line through your design with a thin stream of milk from the pitcher's spout, creating a lovely heart shape. Remember, patience and practice are your faithful companions on this journey.

* **Suggested Image:** A sequence of pictures illustrating the creation of a heart shape in latte art.

Step 4: Expanding Your Portfolio - The Rosetta and the Swan ☕

Once you're confident with the heart, it's time to branch out. The Rosetta and the Swan are classic, elegant designs that are sure to impress. The Rosetta resembles a leaf or fern, while the Swan is exactly what it sounds like - a graceful bird floating on your coffee.

* **Suggested Image:** Side-by-side images of the Rosetta and the Swan designs.

Step 5: Getting Creative - Make Your Masterpiece! 🎨

Now comes the most exciting part - letting your creativity run wild. Try incorporating food coloring, syrups, or chocolate drizzles into your designs. This step really sets apart the amateur from the latte art maestro - are you up for the challenge?

* **Suggested Image:** A latte displaying an intricate, colorful design.

Going Beyond the Basics: Additional Resources 📚

* **Coffee Art Tutorial Videos:** Platforms like YouTube offer an immense library of how-to videos. Watching experts in action can be a great help.
* **Latte Art Classes:** Many specialty coffee shops and schools offer barista courses focusing on latte art.
* **Books on Coffee:** "Coffee Obsession" by Anette Moldvaer and "The World Atlas of Coffee" by James Hoffmann provide a deep dive into the coffee universe.

Your Latte Art Challenge! ☕

Now it's your turn! I challenge you to try these steps and make your own latte art masterpiece. Don't be shy, share your creations with us. The best designs will be featured in our next newsletter. Are you ready to become a latte artist?

Remember, every coffee aficionado started with a spill or two, so let's brew, pour, create, and above all, have fun!

Stay frothy, my friends,

[Your Name]

Coffee is a language in itself, and with a little practice, you too can start speaking latte art! ☕

5. Creation newsletter writing

Now we're onto the creative part.

Here's the prompt:

> *Act as freelance writer, preparing a newsletter.*
>
> *The topic is [topic]*
>
> *The category is [category]*
>
> *Prepare a newsletter issue of 700 words.*
>
> *Include a personal introduction*
>
> *Use bolded section headers*
>
> *Use bullet pointed lists where applicable*
>
> *Do not provide generic information, aim for unique and creative POV.*
>
> *Use a [tone] tone of voice.*
>
> *Make suggestions for images*
>
> *Make suggestions for additional resources*

For [Category] use information from the previous step to generate different types of newsletters.

Prompt Output

Using [topic] = "Exploring Coffee Origins: A Deep Dive into Bean Sourcing"

[category] = "instructional"

[tone of voice] = light, fun

You'll have one of two reactions at the point.

Either:
1. This is excellent
2. This is terrible

Both reactions are great!

If you think the result is excellent then you are good to go. You have your newsletter issue - go ahead and load it into beehiiv or whatever tool you are using.

If you thing the result is terrible then you have a first draft you can start with. Editing is so so so much easier than writing from scratch.

And because you know it's bad that also means you know what would be good. So adjusting should be easy!

Either way you're much closer to having a full issue of the newsletter and it's taken a fraction of the time it would to work from a blank page. You've skipped the awful stage of staring at a blank white screen and a blinking cursor.

Pulling it together

I told you we'd have lots of prompts in this part!

We've covered both content curation and content creation today which is the core of newsletter publishing.

Next will be about refining our issues and starting to build an audience.

Using AI for audience growth

Today is a fun one - we're going to start getting our newsletter out into the world and start audience build.

The basic idea here is to leverage social media networks to grow an audience then use a special technique to get those audience members over into our newsletter list.

1. Creating a name for your Tribe

You have probably noticed in my email newsletter that I start every edition with:

"Hey Prompt Entrepreneur"

This is a conscious decision to carve out a Tribe.
Seth Godin famously introduced this concept into marketing. You can learn more about it here: Seth's Blog.

The short version though is : a Tribe is a group of people connected to one another connected to a leader and connected to an idea.

In our case:

We are connected via Twitter (if you're not come join us here *https://twitter.com/iamkylebalmer*)

I'm the "leader," as much I don't want to be (!), because you are reading this

We are connected around the idea of using AI to start and grow businesses

You need to do the same with your newsletter business. You need to become the leader, the authority, the voice that people want to listen to.

The first part of this is coming up with a name for your tribe. This starts to help people identify.

We use "Prompt Entrepreneurs". That's who we are.

Let's work out your tribe name.

> *Act as Seth Godin, marketing thought leader and author of Tribes.*
>
> *I write a newsletter about [topic]*
>
> *The name of the newsletter is [name of newsletter]*
> *Here is a description of the newsletter:*
>
> *#start description#*
> *[insert newsletter description]*
> *#end description#*
>
> *Give me 10 possible catchy, easy to say Tribe names.*
>
> *Give me a mission statement and a vision statement.*

Plug in details that we created using ChatGPT in Parts 2.

Prompt Output

 Tribe Names:

1. AI Vanguard
2. Tech Titans
3. Algorithm Artisans
4. Prompt Pioneers
5. Data Trailblazers
6. Cognition Catalysts
7. Insight Innovators
8. Synaptic Synergists
9. Intelligence Igniters
10. Neural Navigators

Mission Statement:

Our mission is to empower entrepreneurs, solopreneurs, coaches, and consultants by unveiling the potential of artificial intelligence. We strive to provide actionable, bite-sized insights that will enable businesses to leverage the power of AI, to enhance their operations, marketing and sales. We believe in a future where everyone, irrespective of their technical knowledge, can harness AI to create more impact, with less effort.

Vision Statement:

Our vision is a digital ecosystem where every entrepreneur possesses the knowledge and confidence to apply artificial intelligence in their business practices. We envision a future where the fusion of human creativity and AI-driven insights leads to breakthrough innovations, leveling the playing field for all, and transforming the way online businesses operate. Through 'Prompt Entrepreneur', we aim to be the beacon guiding this change, one email at a time.

This gives me a couple of jumping off points for my Tribe name, as well as some additional information about the mission and vision of the newsletter.

As always ask for more examples if needed. And if they need a tone change say something like "less serious" and you'll get more fun names. That gave me "AI Avengers" which could be a lot of fun - telling my AI Avengers to assemble!

Use this Tribe name in all your newsletters that you publish from now on. And sprinkle it into social media too when relevant.

2. Choosing a social platform

Our best tool in getting initial subscribers, for free, to our newsletter is via social media marketing.

The best tool overall is paid advertising - but that should come later once you've proven the business model and want to scale.

For now we're going to leverage social media using a specific technique we'll develop in the remainder of this part.

There are MANY different techniques you could use but I'm going to give you ONE surefire method to build an audience and gain subscribers.

Act as a social media strategy expert

I want to promote a newsletter called [title] The topic is [topic]

I will be using a DM giveaway as the primary mechanic to build my audience initially.

I am choosing the best social media platform to use.

Provide me with different social platform options, their pros and cons and rank them by attractiveness.

Expand on your top choice in detail.

Prompt Output

 Here are a few social media platform options, their pros and cons, and how they rank in terms of effectiveness for your particular purpose:

1. **LinkedIn**
   Pros: LinkedIn is the leading platform for professional networking, with a large number of entrepreneurs, startups, and business professionals who would likely be interested in a newsletter about AI and business. It's a great place for thought leadership and in-depth discussions.
   Cons: The LinkedIn community often seeks more in-depth content and may not respond as readily to giveaway promotions as other platforms. It might also be more difficult to go viral on LinkedIn due to the nature of the algorithm.
   Rank: 1 – Given your topic, LinkedIn would be the most attractive option because of its professional audience and the relevant interests of that audience.

2. **Twitter**
   Pros: Twitter allows for easy sharing and viral content. There's a strong tech and AI community on Twitter, which could be a potential audience for your newsletter.
   Cons: It can be more challenging to get noticed on Twitter due to the high volume of posts and the rapid pace at which content is shared.
   Rank: 2 – Twitter is a great place for short, sharp messages, and there's a good potential for your message to be shared widely.

3. **Facebook**
   Pros: Facebook has a broad user base and allows for the creation of specialized groups. You could create a group for AI enthusiasts and entrepreneurs and nurture your community there.
   Cons: Organic reach on Facebook has been declining, meaning you might need to use paid promotions to reach a larger audience. Also, it's a more casual social network and may not attract as many serious entrepreneurs or business professionals as LinkedIn or Twitter.
   Rank: 3 – While it's a versatile platform, Facebook may not be as effective for reaching your target audience as LinkedIn or Twitter.

4. **Instagram**
   Pros: Instagram is highly visual and great for brands that have a visual element to promote.
   Cons: It's not as well-suited for professional or tech-related content, and it doesn't support clickable links in posts which can be a hurdle for driving newsletter sign-ups.
   Rank: 4 – Given the focus of your newsletter, Instagram probably wouldn't be the most effective platform to promote it.

This was using my own newsletter and LinkedIn and Twitter are my primary platforms.

I actually use Twitter as primary and LinkedIn as secondary but ChatGPT's analysis is spot on. The high frequency and effort required for Twitter is why ChatGPT chose to put it in #2 instead of #1 but for me personally that's not a problem, hence it being top choice.

Run this analysis on your own newsletter to come up with suggestions.

Still in doubt? Use Twitter. It's the main platform for a lot of growing newsletters. And very likely it will work for you too.

3. The DM giveaway strategy

Building an audience from scratch on any social media platform is difficult. I can't cover a full strategy here, especially for multiple platforms. Well - I could...but for your sanity we're keeping it simple!

Instead we're going to focus on a tried and tested method called a DM giveaway.

The basics are:
- you create something of value.
- you talk about it on social media
- for someone to get it they need to follow you, like your post and comment that they want it
- you DM (direct message) the thing to them

That's sort of it.

It works on all social media platforms but best on Twitter. Especially when combined with tools like *Tweethunter that do the DM'ing for you automatically. *Sign up to Tweethunter here : https://tinyurl.com/ye2x54yy (affiliate link).

It's easier with an example. Here's one I made earlier:

Kyle Balmer | Prompt Ent...

It's here 🎉

New Prompt Playbook.

>Start an Affiliate Marketing Blog with AI<

5000+ words, 18 detailed prompts in a sequenced workflow to build a new income stream

Like and Comment "Blog" below

And I'll DM you the link

Must be following for me to know who to send to

This tweet told people about something of value : a new prompt playbook.

It gives them instructions to follow, like the post and comment Blog on the post.

As soon as they do that they get sent this follow up:

 Kyle Balmer | Prompt Ent...

Thanks for following!

Here's the link :
aspiring-foundation-693.notion.site/Start-an-
Affiliate-Marketing-Blog-with-AI-Prompt-

You can duplicate it to your own Notion or
simply read-only

Any questions or comments shoot me a
message

Also, if you like this you'll love my free daily
newsletter. Join 2000+ AI entrepreneurs at
promptentrepreneur.beehiiv.com

Cheers,

Kyle

What' we've done is:

1. Gain a new follower
2. Gained like + comment engagement on the original tweet (which in turn means it will be seen more)
3. Plugged your newsletter in the DM so people can then subscribe
4. Delivered something valuable to your new audience member so they become a huge fan.

That's the play. Capiche?

It works on Twitter, Facebook, Instagram, LinkedIn or any other platform where you can DM the individual.

I'm going to focus on Twitter because i) it's generally the best platform for newsletter audience growth and ii) there are powerful tools to automate the DM'ing process.

First though: we need something of value to give to audience members!

4. Creating a Lead Magnet

"Lead magnet" is a term we use in online marketing.

It basically means something attractive (like a magnet!) that brings in leads for our business.

An eBook we give away in exchange for an email? That's a lead magnet.

A free consultation in exchange for a telephone number? That's a lead magnet.

A free Notion guide to AI in exchange for a Twitter follow, like and comment? That's a lead magnet.

Lead magnets take a huge amount of forms. But there are similarities.

Lead magnets need to be:
- Valuable to the audience member
- Short and easily consumable

What the exact form and content of the lead magnet will be will depend entirely on your topic and expertise.

Let's use ChatGPT to help us brainstorm some possibilities:

Act as a marketing strategist

Help me create a list of lead magnet ideas for my newsletter

The goal is to get people to engage with my social media content in exchange for this lead magnet.

My topic is [topic]

The lead magnet must be highly valuable, unique not generic and easily consumable (ie. less than 5 minutes to read, watch, listen to)

Give me a list of 10 possible lead magnets including title, format and brief description.

Prompt Output

 Absolutely, here are ten lead magnet ideas that align with your focus of using AI to start a business. These should stimulate engagement with your social media content and encourage sign-ups to your newsletter:

1. **"AI Startup Checklist" (PDF)**: A comprehensive yet concise checklist that guides users through the key considerations when incorporating AI into a startup. Quick to read but packed with actionable advice.
2. **"AI in 5 Minutes: What Every Entrepreneur Should Know" (Video)**: A short, animated explainer video highlighting the key AI concepts every entrepreneur should be aware of. Informative and easily digestible.
3. **"The Pocket Guide to AI Business Terms" (E-Book)**: A compact e-book defining essential AI terminology for business owners. Perfect for quick reference and to increase understanding.
4. **"Cracking the AI Code: 5 Major Misconceptions" (Infographic)**: An engaging infographic that dispels common myths about using AI in business. A valuable resource to inspire confidence in AI adoption.
5. **"5 Key AI Trends for Entrepreneurs" (Podcast Snippet)**: A 5-minute audio extract from a longer podcast episode, discussing the top AI trends that every entrepreneur should follow.
6. **"AI Business Model Canvas" (Interactive PDF)**: A uniquely designed business model canvas tailored for AI startups, allowing entrepreneurs to map out their business plan in a structured, logical way.
7. **"Success Stories: How 5 Businesses Leveraged AI" (Slide Deck)**: A brief but inspiring slide deck showcasing real-world examples of businesses that successfully implemented AI.
8. **"Quick Win AI Tools for Your Business" (Resource List)**: A PDF featuring a list of user-friendly AI tools that entrepreneurs can incorporate into their businesses right now. This offers immediate, practical value.
9. **"Understanding AI Algorithms – Simplified" (Animated GIF series)**: A series of animated GIFs breaking down complex AI algorithms into simple, understandable concepts.
10. **"AI for Your Business in 60 Seconds" (TikTok Style Video Series)**: A series of 60-second, fast-paced videos explaining how AI can revolutionize various aspects of a business.

Each of these options offers a unique value proposition and is tailored to the time constraints of today's busy entrepreneurs. They are designed to provide immediate, actionable value while piquing interest in your newsletter content.

Choose the ones that you like and ask for ChatGPT to expand.

For example I like the first one here. I simply put "Create Option 1" into ChatGPT and get given a checklist to use as my lead magnet.

From there adapt using your own expertise and style. Don't just copy/paste ChatGPT as your lead magnet.

Why? Well: it's lazy.

But also remember this is the first big interaction people will have with you. You need this first interaction to leave them stunned - "wow! they gave away a lot of valuable information here!" Leave a first good impression.

5. Preparing your DM giveaway

Nearly there - we need a handful more elements to launch your giveaway.

Namely:
- Giveaway tweet
- Thank you message
- Optional - automation for DMs

For the giveaway tweet use this prompt to get started:

Act as a [social media platform] engagement expert

Write a post for a DM giveaway post and a thank you message.

##instructions for giveaway post begin##

The giveaway is for this lead magnet:
#begin lead magnet#
[copy/paste text of lead magnet]
#end lead magnet#

To receive the lead magnet they must follow, like the post and comment "DM". Add these details.

##instructions for giveaway post end##

##instructions for thank you message begin##

Write a thank you message that delivers the lead magnet.

Add a thank you

Add a placeholder for me to add a link to the lead magnet

Add a plug for the newsletter [name] with the link [link] suggesting they sign up

Sign off

##instructions for thank you message end##

Replace [social media platform] with whichever platform you are using, ie. Twitter, LinkedIn.

Is your lead magnet video or audio? Copy paste the script in here. It's just to give context to ChatGPT about what the content is.

Prompt Output

 Sure, here's how you can go about it:

Giveaway Post

"🎉 GIVEAWAY ALERT! 🎉

Ready to dive into the world of AI? We're giving away our valuable AI Startup Checklist for FREE to help you take those first successful steps! 🎁

To enter:
1️⃣ Follow @PromptEntrepreneur
2️⃣ Like this tweet
3️⃣ Reply "DM" to this tweet

Act now! Time's ticking, and this exclusive offer won't last forever.

Future AI innovators, your journey starts here! ⭐ #AI #StartUp #Giveaway"

Thank You Message

"Hello there!

Thank you so much for participating in our giveaway! 🙏

We're thrilled to share our exclusive AI Startup Checklist with you. Click on the link below to download it:

[Add the link to the lead magnet here]

We believe it's going to serve you greatly in your journey to building an AI-based business.

For more insightful content and tools, don't forget to sign up for our newsletter, Prompt Entrepreneur. Stay updated and become part of our growing community of AI innovators. Sign up here: [Add newsletter sign-up link]

Thanks again for your interest and engagement. We can't wait to see where your AI journey takes you!

Best,
The Prompt Entrepreneur Team"

From here just plug in the details like the link to the lead magnet. I personally use Notion, which allows me to easily share documents to the web via a public link.

For the actual giveaway you can certainly do it manually, especially initially when volume will be low. Just have your thank you message somewhere easy to access and copy paste it to anyone who signs up.

If you want to automate it though TweetHunter is fantastic. That's what I personally use and recommend it highly.

Pulling it together

In this part we've fleshed out a single tactic for building your audience using social media.

It's my belief that having one strong strategy is better than 10 weak strategies. Don't spread yourself thin.

Instead focus on one thing, get it working and automated, then onto the next.

I'll explore social media platforms and growth in more depth in other guides but right now just nail one audience growth channel using the technique above.

We're moving into the end of the playbook now.

Next is monetisation and howe actually make money from our newsletter. Fun!

Monetization: Advertising and Sponsorships

And here we are at the end of the process.

Over the past 4 Parts we've laid our foundations for growth.

Now I'll talk about how you'll go about monetising your newsletter.

This will be a mix of methods for immediate revenue as well as reviewing the later possibilities so you know what you are aiming for.

1. Recommending other newsletters

The first technique you can immediately start using is generating revenue from each new subscriber you get.

We can do this by recommending other newsletters we think would be helpful for our readers.

An example. I like the newsletter "The Rundown". It's a great breaking news newsletter for AI. Therefore when people sign up for my newsletter I show a quick message that asks if they want to subscribe to "The Rundown".

It looks a bit like this:

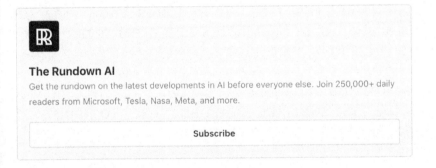

If someone clicks the link, I get paid $1-2. The exact amount depends on the newsletter.

Better, the widget I show has 3 newsletters that I recommend, which means for every new subscriber

I get I can potentially generate 3 x $1-2 or $3 to $6.

It's small but adds up. 10 new subscribers a day could mean $60 of revenue for instance. Pretty cool.

How do we set this up?

In beehiiv it's easy. We use **Boosts**. Go to Monetisation > Boosts and you'll see a list of offers, how much they pay and their terms.

Just choose ones that you think would be genuinely useful for your audience. Make sure to actually read the newsletter! Don't just choose newsletters based on who is paying the most - your brand reputation is more important than this.

Not on beehiiv? No problem - check out Upscribe by Sparkloop. It's free. It requires more manual installation than beehiiv but is a great option if you aren't using beehiiv.

Use recommendations to get your revenue flowing as the first step. It's automatic, easy to implement and no brainer additional cash.

2. Affiliate offers

The next layer of monetisation we add is affiliate offers.

An affiliate offer is basically a link to a product or service that you add to you newsletter. If a reader goes to that link and makes a purchase you, the person who sent them, gets a percentage of the sale.

One of the best known affiliate programmes is Amazon Associates. By becoming an Amazon Associate you can send people to Amazon to buy products. When they buy you make a percentage of that Amazon sale.

If I ran a board gaming newsletter I could review and recommend a board game in my newsletter and add a link to the board game on Amazon.

If someone buys the board game I'd make 6% of the sale. If the board game was $50 I'd make $3. If I drove 100 purchases I'd make $300. Nice.

To check out Amazon's pay out rates check here for USA: Associate Commissions: _https://affiliate-program.amazon.com/_ or Google "your country + Amazon Associates Commission Statement" to find the local rates.

The reason this works well with early stage newsletters is that size doesn't matter. You can join an affiliate programme and drive however many sales - you aren't locked into delivering a certain result. Therefore it's a good early stage revenue stream.

And there are many many affiliate programmes out there. Amazon is one of the largest but we're going to use ChatGPT to find others.

Here's a prompt for starting our affiliate journey:

Act as an affiliate marketing expert.

I write a newsletter about [topic]

Give me a list of known affiliate offers (products and services) in this niche from a wide range of sources like Amazon, Clickbank and other affiliate marketplaces, education marketplaces, individual brands, blogs and influencers

Give me a total of 20 specific known offers

Prompt Output

Using [topic] = board games

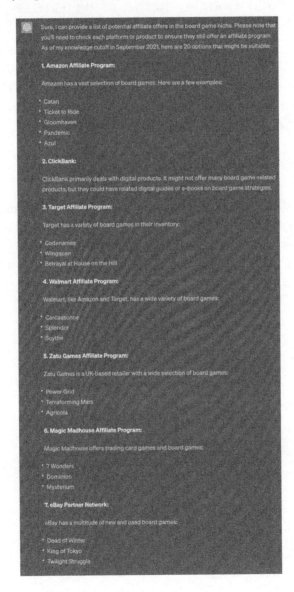

Sure, I can provide a list of potential affiliate offers in the board game niche. Please note that you'll need to check each platform or product to ensure they still offer an affiliate program. As of my knowledge cutoff in September 2021, here are 20 options that might be suitable:

1. Amazon Affiliate Program:

Amazon has a vast selection of board games. Here are a few examples:

* Catan
* Ticket to Ride
* Gloomhaven
* Pandemic
* Azul

2. ClickBank:

ClickBank primarily deals with digital products. It might not offer many board game-related products, but they could have related digital guides or e-books on board game strategies.

3. Target Affiliate Program:

Target has a variety of board games in their inventory:

* Codenames
* Wingspan
* Betrayal at House on the Hill

4. Walmart Affiliate Program:

Walmart, like Amazon and Target, has a wide variety of board games:

* Carcassonne
* Splendor
* Scythe

5. Zatu Games Affiliate Program:

Zatu Games is a UK-based retailer with a wide selection of board games:

* Power Grid
* Terraforming Mars
* Agricola

6. Magic Madhouse Affiliate Program:

Magic Madhouse offers trading card games and board games:

* 7 Wonders
* Dominion
* Mysterium

7. eBay Partner Network:

eBay has a multitude of new and used board games:

* Dead of Winter
* King of Tokyo
* Twilight Struggle

This prompt will give us places to go and check out.

From here visit the websites and find their affiliate programmes. Google "name of website + affiliate" to find the exact page quickly.

From there check their payout rates and terms and conditions. Register for the ones you like the look of to get your affiliate links. Then simply start to drop those links into your upcoming newsletters.

This could be an issue that is specifically a review.

Or it could be a general link to their website - for example I might say "This issue brought to you by Zatu Games" at the top of my site and add my affiliate link straight to their homepage. If they then browse around and make a purchase you'll take a cut.

3. Newsletter Sponsorship

Next up is sponsorship.

This is when a company pays you to feature their product or service.

It could be a link at the top of your newsletter, a small classified advert, a featured piece in the newsletter or even a whole issue takeover.

There are lots of creative ways to do sponsorships but always make sure that it is a positive experience for your readers too!

Generally you'll need a few thousand subscribers before sponsorship makes sense. I've seen newsletters do it with 2000 subscribers in certain niches but generally you'd want to be at 5,000 or ideally 10,000 before it becomes worthwhile for a company to sponsor you.

Act as a sponsorship broker

I publish a newsletter about [topic]

Provide me with a list of companies that might be interested in sponsoring my newsletter.

The companies must match the size of new newsletter. For example a small company will be interested in sponsoring my newsletter when small but a large company will not. I wish to get larger and larger companies as sponsors as I grow.

Provide 5 suggestions for each stage of growth:
1000-5000 subscribers (very small)
5000-10000 subscribers (small)
10000-50000 subscribers (medium)
500000-100000 subscribers (large)
100000+ subscribers (very large)

Provide specific company names

Return everything in tabular format

Prompt Output

Using [topic] = vegan fitness

Subscribers	Potential Sponsors
1000-5000 (Very Small)	1. No Cow (protein bars and snacks) 2. Health Warrior (chia bars) 3. Vivo Life (plant-based supplements) 4. LoveRaw (vegan chocolate) 5. Your Super (superfood mixes)
5000-10000 (Small)	1. Orgain (organic plant-based protein powder) 2. Vegun Nutrition (vegan supplements) 3. MacroLife Naturals (greens and protein powders) 4. iHerb (natural products online retailer) 5. Lenny & Larry's (protein cookies)
10000-50000 (Medium)	1. Vega (plant-based nutrition products) 2. Garden of Life (vitamins and supplements) 3. Sunwarrior (plant-based proteins and supplements) 4. Thrive Market (online natural and organic grocer) 5. Primal Spirit Foods (vegan jerky)
50000-100000 (Large)	1. Puma (launched a vegan sport shoe line) 2. Nature's Path (organic cereals and snacks) 3. Purple Carrot (vegan meal delivery) 4. Silk (plant-based milks) 5. Cliff Bar (energy bars)
100000+ (Very Large)	1. Beyond Meat (plant-based meats) 2. Impossible Foods (plant-based meats) 3. Lululemon (athletic wear) 4. Adidas (launched a line of vegan shoes) 5. Nestlé (has a range of plant-based food products)

Use this a starting list to start reaching out to potential sponsors. At this point it's basically cold outreach via email and LinkedIn until you get some interest.

That's a little too much to go into here so I'll refer you to Email Sponsorship: *https:// emailsponsorship.com/* as a solid resource.

Alternatively you can work with companies that will do outreach for you and help you secure sponsorships. They'll charge a flat monthly fee, take a commission or both.

If you have a strong audience in the right niche this investment is well worth it. Shoot me a tweet or DM (@IamKyleBalmer) and I can provide up to date recommendations here.

4. Advertising

Advertising in the context of newsletters is allowing ads to be inserted directly into your issues.

This is done "programmatically". The ads can change and alter to best fit your audience and (theoretically) lead to more clicks and better performance for your advertisers.

As such this tends to the be most high volume, highest paying source of revenue. It's also nice and automatic, especially compared to securing sponsorships.

However, it means ceding some control over exactly what is shown to your audience. That's a deal breaker for some newsletters.

beehiiv has their own advertising platform directly in the interface: beehiiv Ad Network: _https://www.beehiiv.com/monetize/ad-network_ which makes everything a bit easier.

If using a different newsletter system though then Paved is the big player in this industry.

Pulling it together

In this part we've covered how to start generating revenue from your newsletter.

In brief:
- when you get started roll with newsletter recommendations and affiliate offers
- when you hit 5,000 or 10,000 subscribers (depending on niche) add in sponsorships
- at 10,000 look into programmatic advertising

These four pillars will give you a solid foundation of revenue - automatic low level payments from recommendations and affiliate and more manual big chunks of cash from sponsorships.

And of course as you continue to grow your sign up rate, subscriber count, clicks and sponsorship prices go up so that all of these methods also increase the amount of revenue they are generating.

Recap

Let's review what we've covered:

Part 1: Understanding Newsletters and AI Tools
Part 2: Setting up your newsletter
Part 3: Content Creation with AI - Part 1
Part 4: Content Creation with AI - Audience Building
Part 5: Monetisation: Advertising and Sponsorships

Solid work!

If you run through these past steps you'll have the basic foundations of your newsletter in the right place for growth.

From here it's about consistency and growth. Keep publishing, keep building the audience, keep refining the newsletter based on your audience's feedback.

It will be slow initially. I won't lie to you about that. But the work we've done over the last week has put all your basic systems in place so that this work will pay off if you keep at it.

Have we missed things? Absolutely.

This is because I wanted to give you the bare minimum to get you up and running and creating. Once you are in the world of newsletters you'll find other ways to do things, more ideas for your content, better techniques for growth etc.

Again this is probably the best newsletter growth resource out there so make sure to subscribe:

Newsletter Operator

How to grow and monetize your newsletter. Learn the exact tactics top newsletters are using. Join 8000+ founders, creators, and operators for free.

Subscribe

Subscribe: *https://www.newsletteroperator.com/*

From the foundations we've covered - armed with AI tools to optimise your work - you're in a brilliant position to build a strong, reliable income stream from your writing.

Start an Affiliate Marketing Blog using AI

What is blogging and affiliate marketing?

In short this business revolves around:

Setting up a blog that attracts traffic
Adding "affiliate" links to your content that, when clicked and lead to a purchase, pay you a % of the purchase.

For example if I add an Amazon link to some £120 Birkenstock sandals into one of my blog articles and someone clicks the link, goes to Amazon and purchases I will get 10% or £12 from Amazon.

If I can send 100 people to purchase via that link I will generate £1200.

The key with affiliate marketing is volume, which comes from ranking well on Google which, in turn, depends on having lots of good content on my blog.

Blog articles are the engine that drives affiliate marketing: news, reviews, features, comparisons, in depth breakdowns of products in my affiliate category.

This is one that's near and dear to my heart. My first big blog was *https://learnchinesecharacters.academy/*. A blog site to help people learn Chinese characters. In fact this was my FIRST online business.

Therefore helping others get started in this space is really exciting

Why should I care?

Blogging and affiliate marketing is BIG business According to Statista, affiliate marketing spending in the U.S alone was set to hit $8.2 billion by 2022. Furthermore, a report by Hosting Tribunal reveals that bloggers who earn over $50,000 per year spend an average of 3-10 hours writing a blog post, while 63.2% of those earning over $2000/month invest less than 3 hours.

You're probably thinking: "That sounds amazing, but how do I keep up with the constant demand for fresh content?" A blog needs to be fed with LOTS of new, fresh, quality content for Google to take notice.

Enter ChatGPT.

With ChatGPT, you can create quality content faster and more efficiently, allowing you to stay ahead of the curve, and offering you a competitive edge in today's fast-paced digital environment.

ChatGPT means that affiliate marketing is at an inflection point where business owners who use AI can outstrip business owners who do not.

And I'm not just talking about blog writing - ChatGPT can be used at all points in the set up and operation of an affiliate marketing focused blog.
And that's just what we're going to show you this week!

Structure of the guide

It's going to be a busy week. But by the end you'll have the structure, system and prompts to launch your own affiliate blog. In brief here's the week:

Part 1: Market Research and Niche Selection: This stage involves identifying your interests and passions, conducting keyword research to understand what potential readers are searching for, analysing your competition to identify their strengths and weaknesses, and validating your chosen niche to ensure there's a viable market and potential for monetization.

Part 2: Blog Setup and Design: This stage involves choosing a blogging platform, selecting a domain name that's relevant and easy to remember and designing a brand.

Part 3: Content Creation with ChatGPT: This stage involves developing a content strategy and calendar, using ChatGPT to generate content such as blog posts, outlines, and new content ideas, editing and optimizing the content for accuracy, style, voice, and SEO, and including affiliate links in a natural, non-spammy way.

Part 4: Promotion, SEO, and Link Building with ChatGPT: This stage involves using ChatGPT to generate SEO-friendly meta descriptions, title tags, and alt text for images, promoting your blog posts on social media, building an email list and sending regular newsletters, reaching out to other bloggers for guest posting opportunities and link building, and monitoring and adjusting your strategy based on your blog's performance data.

Let's get started.

Market Research and Niche Selection

1. Identify Your Interests and Passions

The first step is to identify what you're passionate about. This could be anything from cooking to technology to fitness.

Here is an initial ChatGPT prompt to start brainstorming topics:

> *As a brainstorming assistant, generate a list of potential blog niches based on my interests in [insert interests here].*
>
> *The goal is to come up with unique and engaging niches that combine these interests. Combine interests where they naturally intersect but do not force combination. Please avoid overly wide niches.*

Plug in interests, your work area, skills, hobbies. Anything that is important to you.

It's important that we start from a basis of what you actually want to write about if we want to create a unique and genuinely interesting blog.

Yes, we'll be using AI to help with writing later but we need the personal touch from working with a topic we want to write about and have the authority to write about.

Prompt Output

1. "AI-Powered Fitness: Exploring the Intersection of Machine Learning and Weightlifting"
   * This blog would focus on the advancements of AI in the fitness industry, including how AI can help with workout optimization, personal training, nutrition, and more.
2. "Techpreneur's Journey: From Coding AI to Building Startups"
   * This blog would share insights about the entrepreneurial journey in the tech industry, particularly AI. It could include practical advice, interviews with successful techpreneurs, and updates about the AI industry.
3. "Gaming for Growth: Personal Development through Video Games"
   * Explore how video games can contribute to personal development. Discuss video game design, the psychology behind gaming, and the potential benefits of gaming such as improving problem-solving skills, decision-making abilities, and social skills.
4. "AI in Gaming: The Future of Interactive Entertainment"
   * This blog would delve into the intersection of AI and video games, discussing how AI is shaping the future of gaming, from NPC behavior to game design and personalization.
5. "Entrepreneurial Fitness: Balancing Startups and Weightlifting"
   * Discuss how fitness, particularly weightlifting, can complement the entrepreneurial lifestyle. You could cover topics such as maintaining a consistent workout schedule despite a busy work life, the benefits of exercise for mental clarity, and more.
6. "Lifting and Leadership: Strength Training Lessons for Entrepreneurship"
   * Draw parallels between weightlifting principles (e.g., discipline, progressive overload, resilience) and running a successful business. Discuss how lessons learned from weightlifting can be applied to entrepreneurship.
7. "Machines & Muscles: AI Analysis of Weightlifting Techniques"
   * This blog could focus on how AI can analyze and improve weightlifting techniques, postures, and routines for maximum efficiency and safety.
8. "Gamified Fitness: Leveraging Video Game Mechanics in Weightlifting"
   * Discuss the application of gaming principles and mechanics in the fitness world, for instance, VR/AR integration into workouts, fitness apps with gaming elements, etc.
9. "Better Self with AI: Exploring AI Applications in Personal Development"
   * Delve into the role of AI in personal development, from AI-driven meditation apps to AI coaches for habit formation and other areas of personal growth.
10. "Startup Game: Entrepreneurial Lessons from the Video Game Industry"

   * Explore the business and entrepreneurial side of the video game industry, discussing how video game startups navigate the market, the role of innovation, and lessons that can be applied to other industries.

Each of these niches has its own unique angle and caters to a specific audience, yet all of

2. Conduct Keyword Research

Once you've identified your niche, it's time to conduct keyword research. This will help you understand what potential readers in your niche are searching for.

Keywords are basically how people use Google - their search terms.

You can use tools like Google Keyword Planner, SEMrush, or Ahrefs, or you can ask ChatGPT to get started.

As a SEO assistant, suggest a list of potential keywords for a blog focused on [topic]. The task involves identifying high-volume, low-competition keywords.

The goal is to find keywords that can drive organic traffic to the blog. Please avoid extremely competitive keywords.

For topic take the topic you've decided upon from the first step. Or plug in the whole answer that ChatGPT gave you (with title, description etc.) to get even more detail.

Prompt Output

 As an AI, I don't have real-time access to SEO tools or databases to identify the current keyword trends or competition levels, but I can suggest some keywords based on your niche and general SEO knowledge. Once you have the keywords, you can use a tool like Google's Keyword Planner, SEMRush, or Ahrefs to check the search volume and competition.

For the blog niche "Entrepreneurial Fitness: Balancing Startups and Weightlifting", here are some keyword suggestions:

1. Entrepreneur fitness routine
2. Fitness for entrepreneurs
3. Startups and fitness
4. Entrepreneur workout schedule
5. Health tips for entrepreneurs
6. Weightlifting for busy professionals
7. Exercise for startup founders
8. How to balance fitness with work
9. Productivity and fitness
10. Fitness tips for business owners
11. Workout routines for busy entrepreneurs
12. Exercise and entrepreneurship
13. Weightlifting benefits for entrepreneurs
14. Time management for fitness and work
15. Fitness and mental clarity for business
16. Stress management for entrepreneurs through fitness
17. Fitness and success in business
18. Fitness apps for entrepreneurs
19. Health and wellness for startups
20. Fitness strategies for entrepreneurs

Remember to create long-tail keywords based on these suggestions, which can have lower

Pro Tips|
- For better results use the ChatGPT plugin SERPstat SEO tool to use live data. Requires paid ChatGPT plan
- Alternatively take your keywords to Google Ads Keyword planner - *https://ads.google.com/home/tools/keyword-planner/* to get precise keyword volume and competition. Free tool.
- Also plug your topic into Answer the Public - *https://answerthepublic.com/* to start to widen your keywords and see the sort of blog topics you could be writing.

3. Analyze Your Competition

Understanding your competition is crucial. Look at the top blogs in your chosen niche. What are they doing well? What can you do better or differently? ChatGPT can help with this:

As a competitive analysis assistant, provide an analysis of the top three blogs in the [topic] niche. The task involves identifying their strengths, weaknesses, and unique selling points.

The goal is to understand what they're doing well and where there are opportunities for differentiation.

Please avoid personal opinions and stick to objective analysis. Present results in a table.

Prompt Output

Using [entrepreneurship and fitness] as the niche:

Here is a table featuring a high-level analysis of these blogs.

	Foundr	Tim Ferriss	Nerd Fitness
Strengths	Rich, engaging, and actionable content. Regular expert interviews. Strong social media presence.	Wide content variety - not just entrepreneurship and fitness but also lifestyle, psychology, etc. High-profile interviews.	Specific focus on fitness for beginners. Strong community aspect (forums, events).
Weaknesses	Mostly digital entrepreneurship focused. Limited physical fitness content.	Some readers might find content too diverse, losing focus on a single area.	Lacks content on entrepreneurship.
Unique Selling Point	Extensive resources for digital startups, including podcasts and online courses.	Diverse content, from quick tips to long-form articles and interviews, leveraging Ferriss' wide network.	Combines fitness with "nerd" culture, catering to a niche audience.

Prompt Output

Make sure to add in the [topic] in the prompt and hit enter.

ChatGPT will then ask for details for each of the 5 courses.

If you provide information but ChatGPT is still missing info it will prompt you for more.

Keep going until you've added information about all 5 courses. Then ChatGPT will begin its analysis. It may need to be told to begin the analysis after the 5th course- just say "start" or "ok" and it'll begin.

The output will look like this:

Here is a table featuring a high-level analysis of these blogs.

	Foundr	Tim Ferriss	Nerd Fitness
Strengths	Rich, engaging, and actionable content. Regular expert interviews. Strong social media presence.	Wide content variety - not just entrepreneurship and fitness but also lifestyle, psychology, etc. High-profile interviews.	Specific focus on fitness for beginners. Strong community aspect (forums, events).
Weaknesses	Mostly digital entrepreneurship focused. Limited physical fitness content.	Some readers might find content too diverse, losing focus on a single area.	Lacks content on entrepreneurship.
Unique Selling Point	Extensive resources for digital startups, including podcasts and online courses.	Diverse content, from quick tips to long-form articles and interviews, leveraging Ferriss' wide network.	Combines fitness with "nerd" culture, catering to a niche audience.

This gives us a comparative analysis of the top 5 Udemy courses in our niche.

Because these are the top 5 they are doing something right - we want to learn from them. So this is invaluable information. In the next step we'll go a little further with this competitive intelligence.

4. Validate Your Niche

Finally, you need to validate your chosen niche. Is there an audience for your topic? Are there affiliate programs available?

ChatGPT can assist with this validation:

> As a market research assistant, validate the potential of the entrepreneurship and fitness niche. The task involves identifying the size of the audience, potential for monetisation, and availability of affiliate programs.
>
> The goal is to ensure there's a viable market for this
> blog. Please avoid assumptions and use data-driven insights.

Prompt Output

Audience Size:

In the U.S alone, approximately 27 million people are self-identified entrepreneurs, and the interest in entrepreneurship continues to grow, especially due to the trend towards remote and flexible working, which has been intensified by the COVID-19 pandemic.

Regarding fitness, a study by the Physical Activity Council suggested that nearly 64% of Americans aged 6 and above participated in a physical activity in 2020. Fitness is a wide niche, with various sub-niches, including home workouts, gym training, yoga, pilates, running, etc.

Monetization Potential:

Both entrepreneurship and fitness are highly monetizable sectors.

In entrepreneurship, common monetization methods include courses, eBooks, consulting services, sponsorships, and ads. As per 2021, the eLearning market alone was expected to reach $374.3 billion by 2026, indicating the potential for online courses.

The fitness industry has a wide array of products for monetization - workout gear, supplements, exercise programs, meal plans, fitness apps, etc. The global fitness and health club industry generated more than 96.7 billion U.S. dollars in revenue in 2019.

Affiliate Programs:

There are several affiliate programs available in both niches.

Entrepreneurship programs include those offered by online course platforms (like Coursera, Udemy), book sellers (Amazon), and software tools (Shopify, ClickFunnels).

Fitness programs can involve equipment (Amazon, Rogue Fitness), supplements (BodyBuilding.com), digital workout platforms (Beachbody), and meal plans or food delivery services (HelloFresh).

While these are promising factors, I must stress that the success of a blog in these niches will greatly depend on the quality of content, the ability to drive traffic and convert that traffic into revenue. Additionally, the landscape may have changed post my last training data in September 2021, so current market research is advised.

Pulling it together

These four prompts will get your started with defining what exactly your blog is going to be about.

We started with your skills and interests, combined this with keyword research to convert into "Google speak" then checked competition and business viability.

If the results from ChatGPT aren't encouraging (especially in prompt 4!) go back and tweak your variables until you land on something more promising.

It's super important to have a strong, exciting idea that *also* has a market for you build a business. Getting this stage right will make the rest of the process much easier!

Blog Setup
and Design

1. Choose your blogging platform

First up we need to chose what we're building our blog on.

ChatGPT is not going to build our blog for us. That's not what it's for.

Instead we can use ChatGPT to explore options and make suggestions based on our personal circumstances.

> As a affiliate marketing advisor, walk me through my choice of the best blogging platform.
> Ask me questions about my budget, my technical experience and how much time I can commit to this project.
>
> Possible blog platforms include but are not limited to Wordpress self-hosted, Wordpress.com, Medium, Ghost, Wix, Squarespace, Weebly, Blogger, Substack and beehiiv.
>
> SEO is important for this blog. Traffic will come from Google SEO primarily and social media secondarily.
>
> Return your ranking of results in order of highest to lowest preference based on my responses, with pros and cons of each platform, in a table.

This prompt will run you through a similar set of questions to what I would personally ask you if we were sitting together.

This helps narrow down the potential blogging platform. Supplement this with your own research of course!

If you want a quick answer though - if you are good at tech go with self-hosted Wordpress + an Elementor theme. If you are not good at tech go with beehiiv (if you are also interested in a newsletter at some point - and it makes sense for your niche) or Wordpress .com (if you don't want a newsletter).

Prompt Output

Based on your preferences, I recommend considering the following blogging platforms ranked in order of preference:

1. WordPress.com
2. Medium
3. Ghost
4. Substack
5. Blogger

Here is a table summarizing the pros and cons of each platform:

Platform	Pros	Cons
WordPress.com	Easy to set up and use, managed hosting, built-in monetization options through WordAds	Limited customization options, limited plugin support
Medium	Wide reach and exposure to the Medium community, clean and minimalistic design, built-in monetization program	Limited control over design and branding, potential changes to Medium's policies
Ghost	Modern and minimalist design, focused on writing experience, SEO-friendly, built-in membership and subscription features	Requires technical setup and maintenance, limited plugin options compared to WordPress
Substack	Built-in monetization features, user-friendly interface, email newsletter integration	Primarily designed for newsletters, limited customization options for blog layout
Blogger	Simple and easy to use, free hosting, integration with Google services, potential for monetization through AdSense	Limited design options, outdated interface, not as feature-rich as other platforms

These platforms offer a minimalistic design, free options, and built-in monetization features that align with your requirements for affiliate marketing. Each platform has its own strengths and considerations, so I recommend exploring them further to determine which one best suits your specific needs.

Remember to assess factors such as ease of use, customization options, community engagement, and additional features that may be relevant to your affiliate marketing strategy.

2. Naming your blog

Next we're going to generate a killer name for our affiliate blog.

Use the prompt below to generate a list of names.

Plug in your niche and top 2-3 keywords from the previous Step 1.

> *Act as a marketing consultant. Generate 20 potential business names My business is a blog that is focused on [niche] We provide educational content, news and reviews Use the following keywords as inspiration: [copy paste top keywords] Ideally the business name should incorporate a top keyphrase but also generate ideas outside of these keyphrases Focus on easy to say and write names using simple language that works for SEO Keep the business name to 2-3 words maximum*

Prompt Output

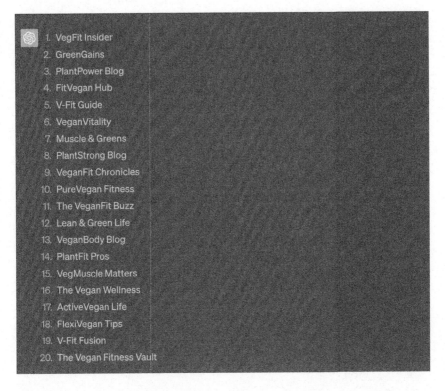

1. VegFit Insider
2. GreenGains
3. PlantPower Blog
4. FitVegan Hub
5. V-Fit Guide
6. VeganVitality
7. Muscle & Greens
8. PlantStrong Blog
9. VeganFit Chronicles
10. PureVegan Fitness
11. The VeganFit Buzz
12. Lean & Green Life
13. VeganBody Blog
14. PlantFit Pros
15. VegMuscle Matters
16. The Vegan Wellness
17. ActiveVegan Life
18. FlexiVegan Tips
19. V-Fit Fusion
20. The Vegan Fitness Vault

Once you've generated a list of names go through and choose the ones you like the sound of.

If you need more just enter "more" into ChatGPT.

If you want a different style, for instance more professional sounding, go ahead and tell ChatGPT: "more professional".

Continue doing this until you have 10+ names that you like.

Next step is to go to *https://www.namecheckr.com/*

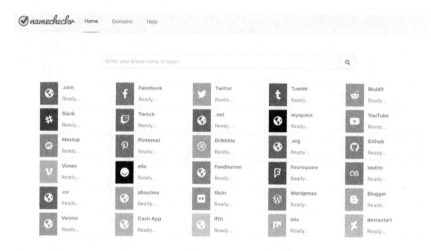

This website lets you check name availability on multiple platforms at once. Plug your business name in to see if it's available.

You are looking for name that is available on:
- .com
- Facebook
- Twitter
- Instagram
- Youtube

And TikTok, which you need to check manually.

Once you've found a name that i) you love and ii) is available on all or most platforms you're good to go.

3. Brand guidelines

Now we have a name let's flesh out the brand a bit by building up some brand guidlines.

Here's the prompt:

> *Act as a branding consultant*
> *Prepare a set of brand guidelines for an affiliate blog in [niche] The name of the blog is [name of blog] The main keywords the blog will be ranking for are [top keywords]*
>
> *Provide me with a brand description, elevator pitch, target market, brand promise, brand mission, value proposition, brand voice/personality and brand culture.*

As always, plug in your specific details.

Notice how we are using results from previous steps in each new prompt - we're iterating and adding more detail each time.

Prompt Output

Brand Description:
Muscle & Greens is an empowering affiliate blog that combines the best of vegan nutrition and fitness to help individuals achieve their fitness goals while embracing a compassionate and sustainable lifestyle. We believe in the power of plant-based living to fuel muscle growth and optimize workouts, and we are dedicated to providing valuable resources, insightful content, and trusted product recommendations for the vegan fitness community.

Elevator Pitch:
Muscle & Greens is the ultimate destination for vegans who are passionate about fitness. We offer a wealth of expert advice, evidence-based information, and curated product recommendations to help you build muscle, enhance your workouts, and excel in your fitness journey, all while staying true to your plant-based values.

Target Market:
Our target market includes health-conscious individuals who follow a vegan lifestyle and have a keen interest in fitness. They are motivated to build muscle, improve their athletic performance, and maintain a balanced and sustainable approach to their overall well-being. Our audience comprises a wide range of age groups, from young adults to middle-aged individuals, who are seeking reliable and practical guidance in the realm of vegan fitness.

Brand Promise:
At Muscle & Greens, we promise to empower our audience with the knowledge, resources, and inspiration they need to thrive in their vegan fitness journey. We are committed to delivering reliable, evidence-based information, recommending high-quality vegan fitness products, and fostering a supportive community that shares the same passion for a plant-powered, active lifestyle.

Brand Mission:
Our mission is to bridge the gap between veganism and fitness by providing a comprehensive platform that educates, motivates, and supports individuals in achieving their fitness goals without compromising their ethical choices. We strive to break stereotypes and show that a plant-based diet can be the foundation for optimal muscle growth, improved athletic performance, and overall health and wellness.

Value Proposition:
Muscle & Greens offers a unique blend of vegan nutrition expertise and fitness knowledge to help individuals unlock their true potential. By choosing our brand, our audience gains access to carefully curated content, reliable product recommendations, and a supportive community that shares their values. We are the go-to resource for vegan fitness enthusiasts who want to optimize their workouts, fuel muscle growth, and lead a sustainable lifestyle.

Brand Voice/Personality:
The Muscle & Greens brand voice is informative, approachable, and inspirational. We strive to communicate with authority and credibility while maintaining a friendly and supportive tone. We celebrate progress, encourage self-belief, and foster a sense of community among our audience. Our language is inclusive, empowering, and rooted in the belief that anyone can achieve their fitness goals through a plant-based lifestyle.

Brand Culture:
Muscle & Greens cultivates a culture of authenticity, transparency, and continuous learning. We value the diverse perspectives and experiences within the vegan fitness community and encourage open dialogue and knowledge sharing. We are committed to staying up to date with the latest research, trends, and innovations in vegan nutrition and fitness, and we proactively adapt our content and recommendations to ensure our audience receives the most valuable and accurate information.

Adjust as required, specifying changes directly to ChatGPT until you are happy with each section.

4. Basic copy

We've got our blogging platform decided. We've chosen a name. We've got some brand guidelines.

Go ahead and set up the basics of your blog. If you need instructions on how try "steps to set up an affiliate blog on PLATFORM NAME" in ChatGPT or head to Google/Youtube to follow some tutorials.

Whichever platform you chose we're going to need some basic "copy".

Copy is short for copywriting and is basically text about our business.

We're going to use this copy in lots of places: our website, on our social media accounts. Basically generating a whole load of copy that be plugged into your blog and social media whenever needed.

Act as a marketing copywriter

The affiliate blog's topic is [niche] Create copy for my affiliate blog named [blog name] The primary keywords are [top keywords] Incorporate information from these brand guidelines #brand guidelines begin# [copy/ paste brand guidelines] #brand guidelines end#

Use this information to generate

Company slogan Tagline Blog home page headlines x 5 Blog home page subheadline x5

Primary features/benefits of the blog Page meta description Twitter bio description Instagram description Facebook page description LinkedIn Page About Us description Tiktok description

Provide results in tabular format

Prompt Output

Element	Copy
Company Slogan	Fuel Your Vegan Fitness Journey
Tagline	Power Your Workouts, Nourish Your Muscles
Blog Home Page Headline 1	Unlock the Potential of Vegan Fitness
Blog Home Page Headline 2	Elevate Your Workouts with Plant-Powered Nutrition
Blog Home Page Headline 3	Discover the Secrets of Vegan Muscle Growth
Blog Home Page Headline 4	Your Guide to Thriving in Vegan Fitness
Blog Home Page Headline 5	Empower Your Body with Muscle & Greens
Blog Home Page Subheadline 1	Expert advice, practical tips, and in-depth guides for vegan fitness enthusiasts
Blog Home Page Subheadline 2	Explore the intersection of plant-based living and athletic performance
Blog Home Page Subheadline 3	Unleash the power of vegan nutrition for optimal muscle growth
Blog Home Page Subheadline 4	Embrace a compassionate lifestyle without compromising your fitness goals
Blog Home Page Subheadline 5	Join a supportive community of like-minded vegan fitness enthusiasts
Primary Features/Benefits	1. Evidence-based information for vegan fitness 2. Curated product recommendations 3. Supportive community of like-minded individuals 4. Practical tips and guidance for building muscle 5. Insights into the power of plant-based living for workouts
Page Meta Description	Fuel your vegan fitness journey with Muscle & Greens. Discover expert advice, evidence-based information, and curated product recommendations to optimize your workouts and unlock your muscle growth potential while embracing a compassionate and sustainable lifestyle. Join our supportive community of like-minded individuals today.
Twitter Bio Description	Empowering vegan fitness enthusiasts with expert advice, evidence-based information, and product recommendations for optimal muscle growth. Join our supportive community and fuel your fitness journey with Muscle & Greens.
Instagram Description	Your go-to resource for vegan fitness. Fuel your workouts, nourish your muscles, and embrace a compassionate lifestyle with Muscle & Greens. Join our community today.
Facebook Page Description	Muscle & Greens is a trusted affiliate blog that combines vegan nutrition and fitness expertise. Discover evidence-based advice, curated product recommendations, and a supportive community of like-minded individuals. Fuel your fitness journey with us.
LinkedIn Page About Us Description	Muscle & Greens bridges the gap between veganism and fitness, empowering individuals to achieve their fitness goals while staying true to their ethical choices. We provide reliable information, curated product recommendations, and foster a supportive community. Join us in optimizing workouts, fueling muscle growth, and promoting a sustainable lifestyle.
TikTok Description	Unlock the power of vegan fitness with Muscle & Greens. Follow us for expert tips, inspiring content, and practical advice on building muscle, enhancing workouts, and embracing a plant-based lifestyle. Join our community today.

Need additional specific copy? Use the same prompt + details and just change the outputs you want.

5. Logo design

Wrapping up today we're going to generate instructions for a brand logo.

Here's the prompt:

> *Act as a visual designer*
> *Based on the provided brand guidelines describe 5 logo ideas*
>
> *The company name is [company name] and should be the only text in the logo*
>
> *#brand guidelines begin#*
> *[copy/paste brand guidelines]*
> *#brand guidelines end#*
>
> *Provide logo description, colors with hex code, text font and size if included. These descriptions will be used as creative briefs so be exhaustive in your details*
>
> *Provide in tabular format*

Prompt Output

Logo Idea	Description	Colors (Hex Codes)	Text Font	Text Size
Idea 1: Leafy Muscle	This logo features a bold and prominent leaf-shaped muscle symbol, combining the concepts of plant-based nutrition and strength. The leafy muscle is designed in vibrant green color, representing vitality and health. The typography is clean and modern, with the words "Muscle & Greens" placed below the symbol, creating a balanced composition.	Green: #00A99D	Montserrat (Bold)	48pt
Idea 2: Strength Leaf	This logo incorporates a stylized leaf-shaped symbol that portrays strength and power. The symbol is rendered in a gradient of green, symbolizing growth and energy. The typography is simple yet impactful, with the company name "Muscle & Greens" placed beside the symbol, creating a cohesive visual identity.	Green Gradient: #7BC96F, #3CA581	Poppins (Medium)	48pt
Idea 3: Green Compass	This logo combines a circular compass symbol with a leaf, representing the brand's commitment to providing guidance and support in the realm of vegan fitness. The compass is depicted in green color, while the leaf adds an element of nature and sustainability. The typography is clear and legible, with the company name "Muscle & Greens" positioned below the symbol.	Green: #3CA581	Lato (Regular)	36pt
Idea 4: Vital Leaf	This logo features a vibrant and energetic leaf symbol, emphasizing the connection between plant-based living and vitality. The leaf is designed in a gradient of green, symbolizing health and growth. The typography is bold and modern, with the company name "Muscle & Greens" integrated with the symbol, creating a unified and impactful logo.	Green Gradient: #4FBF75, #37A366	Roboto (Bold)	48pt
Idea 5: Green Momentum	This logo incorporates an abstract arrow symbol composed of leaf-shaped elements, symbolizing the momentum and progress achieved through a vegan fitness lifestyle. The arrow is rendered in shades of green, creating a sense of movement and energy. The typography is bold and impactful, with the company name "Muscle & Greens" positioned alongside the symbol, forming a cohesive visual identity.	Green Shades: #8ACDA8, #55937E	Oswald (Bold)	48pt

Now that we have a text description we have a few options.

First up you can hire a designer on Fiverr or Upwork to design the logo for you. Provide them with your logo specification as a starting point.

Alternatively you can use an AI generator to create your logo. Here's Midjourney's attempt of the first logo (Leafy Muscle):

You'll notice that Midjourney is good at the visual elements but not the text elements! So these would need to be edited to adjust the

text. If you're good with Photoshop this is strong alternative.

Teaching how to set up Midjourney is beyond this guide. Here's the _quick start guide_.

Pulling it together

Wow!

We've got a LOT done in these past 5 prompts.

You now have the basics of your brand ready. Go ahead and plug all these details in your blog platform of choice.

We've now done the main setup for the business: deciding the niche and setting up the brand basics.

Good job!

Content Creation with ChatGPT

1. Develop a Content Strategy

First up we're going to have ChatGPT help work out our high level content strategy.

We're borrowing an SEO concept called content pillars: in short having a range of content all grouped into categories.

We're then asking for blog types within these pillars: for instance reviews, testimonials, expert advice.

Here's the prompt:

Act as a affiliate marketing expert. Help me to design a content strategy for my affiliate marketing blog.

The category is [niche]

My keywords are [copy/paste keywords]

Provide 5 content pillars

Provide 3 blog formats per content pillar, each should be text, no video or image based content

Give examples of each of the content types for each of the 5 content pillars for a total of 15 content pillar/format combinations

Take into account these brand guidelines in your response

#begin brand guidelines#
[copy/paste brand guidelines]
#end brand guidelines#

Provide everything in tabular format

Plug in your niche and top keywords to customise the prompt to your needs.

Also drop in your brand guidelines to help ChatGPT modify suggestions. For instance if your brand is focused on ethical consumption and organic goods this will be added into your content strategy.

Prompt Output

Absolutely, here's a tailored content strategy for your vegan fitness blog with the keywords you specified:

Content Pillar	Blog Format	Examples
1. Vegan Protein Sources	How-to Guides	"How to Incorporate High Protein Vegan Foods for Muscle Growth"
	Comparative Reviews	"Pea Protein vs. Soy Protein: Which is Better for Vegan Muscle Growth?"
	Listicles	"Top 10 Protein-Rich Foods for Vegan Bodybuilders"
2. Vegan Fitness Routines	How-to Guides	"How to Create a Vegan Fitness Routine for Bodybuilding"
	Personal Narratives	"My Journey to Fitness: A Vegan Bodybuilder's Workout Routine"
	Listicles	"7 Vegan-Friendly Exercises for Maximum Muscle Growth"
3. Vegan Diet and Nutrition	How-to Guides	"How to Plan Your Vegan Diet for Optimal Fitness and Bodybuilding"
	Expert Interviews	"Discussing Vegan Fitness Nutrition with a Renowned Dietitian"
	Listicles	"The Top 10 Nutrients Every Vegan Bodybuilder Needs"
4. Vegan Bodybuilding Success Stories	Personal Narratives	"How I Built Muscle on a Vegan Diet: A Personal Journey"
	Case Studies	"From Average to Athlete: A Vegan Bodybuilder's Success Story"
	Expert Interviews	"Interview with a Champion: Secrets of a Successful Vegan Bodybuilder"
5. Vegan Fitness Products and Supplements	Product Reviews	"Review: The Best Vegan Protein Powders for Bodybuilding"
	How-to Guides	"How to Select the Right Vegan Supplements for Your Fitness Goals"
	Listicles	"The Top 5 Vegan Supplements for Bodybuilding: A Comprehensive Review"

This content strategy provides a diverse range of topics and formats, which should engage your audience and optimize your blog for your target keywords.

As always if any content pillar or blog format doesn't interest you ask ChatGPT to make the appropriate changes. When happy we'll be using this strategy in the next step.

2. Article Title Brainstorm

Armed with our content strategy we're now going to have ChatGPT come up with blog titles.

The blog titles are the first step in SEO and generating traffic - the titles will be the starting point for the actual blog articles themselves. So we need great blog titles first and foremost.

As an affiliate marketing expert use the provide content strategy to generate blog titles for my affiliate blog

My blog is focused on [niche]

My top keywords are [top keywords]

I will provide you with a content strategy which contains 5 Content pillars, each of which has 3 blog formats for a total of 15 combinations.

For each of the combinations generate 20 potential SEO optimised and clickable blog titles. Keep each title between 50-60 characters optimally.

Provide results in list format.

#content strategy begins#
[copy/paste content strategy]
#content strategy ends#

Prompt Output

This prompt is going to kick out a LOT of information. 300 blog titles in fact.

Here's the output for just one of the content pillars:

This is 20 blog titles per format type. And there are 3 format types per content pillar. For a total of 300 blog article titles.

This is going to give you and extremely wide range of coverage for SEO *and* will lead to interesting and readable content.

We could have just asked for 300 blog articles about one topic - that might be good for Google SEO.

But imagine how boring that blog is going to be for actual human readers. Very!

So instead we are building up an interesting base of content pillars and format types for variety.

We're now going to take these blog titles into blog creation.

3. Blog post creation

First up - the elephant in the room. SEO and AI.

Lots of people say that AI content will not work for SEO because Google will eventually deprioritise it and stop showing it to visitors.

This is true.

If I just went into ChatGPT and said "write me a blog post on vegan protein sources". ChatGPT would create something generic that sounds very "AI".
Try it now! The results will be rubbish.

But what we've been doing up, through these multiple steps, is building up material so that our blog posts will be unique and undetectable as AI generated.

We started in Part 1 with keyword research and choosing our niche. In Part 2 we built on this with a name and brand guidelines, which were *built on* Part 1.

We've now folded all of this information from Part 1 and 2 into today's work - our content strategy and blog titles are based on the brand guidelines which in turn are based on prior work!

See what we've been doing? Each time we build on past work we're making the results more and more unique. This is why it's important to go step by step, always using outputs from the previous work in new prompts.

Now we're going to use all of this to generate *unique, interesting and undetectable* SEO optimised articles.

Here's the prompt:

Act as a SEO blog writer.

Write a 750-1000 word SEO optimised blog article with the title : [title]. Optimise the article for keyphrases in the title.

This is a [blog format] article

Use the AIDA writing framework

Use subheadings, bullet points and make suggestions for images when appropriate

Implement the following brand guidelines, paying special attention to the tone of voice

#brand guidlines begin#
[copy/paste brand guidelines]
#brand guidelines end#

Prompt Output

This will kick out an entire blog article for you. Here it is, apologies for the size!

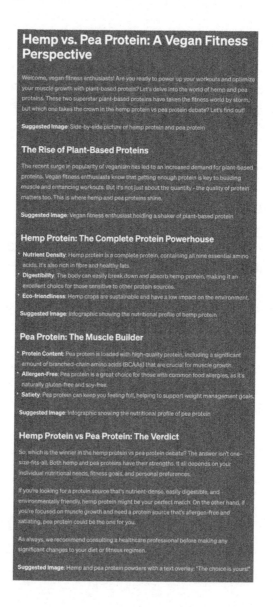

Hemp vs. Pea Protein: A Vegan Fitness Perspective

Welcome, vegan fitness enthusiasts! Are you ready to power up your workouts and optimize your muscle growth with plant-based protein? Let's delve into the world of hemp and pea proteins. These two superstar plant-based proteins have taken the fitness world by storm, but which one takes the crown in the hemp protein vs pea protein debate? Let's find out!

Suggested Image: Side-by-side picture of hemp protein and pea protein

The Rise of Plant-Based Proteins

The recent surge in popularity of veganism has led to an increased demand for plant-based proteins. Vegan fitness enthusiasts know that getting enough protein is key to building muscle and enhancing workouts. But it's not just about the quantity - the quality of protein matters too. This is where hemp and pea proteins shine.

Suggested Image: Vegan fitness enthusiast holding a shaker of plant-based protein

Hemp Protein: The Complete Protein Powerhouse

* **Nutrient Density:** Hemp protein is a complete protein, containing all nine essential amino acids. It's also rich in fibre and healthy fats.
* **Digestibility:** The body can easily break down and absorb hemp protein, making it an excellent choice for those sensitive to other protein sources.
* **Eco-friendliness:** Hemp crops are sustainable and have a low impact on the environment.

Suggested Image: Infographic showing the nutritional profile of hemp protein

Pea Protein: The Muscle Builder

* **Protein Content:** Pea protein is loaded with high-quality protein, including a significant amount of branched-chain amino acids (BCAAs) that are crucial for muscle growth.
* **Allergen-Free:** Pea protein is a great choice for those with common food allergies, as it's naturally gluten-free and soy-free.
* **Satiety:** Pea protein can keep you feeling full, helping to support weight management goals.

Suggested Image: Infographic showing the nutritional profile of pea protein

Hemp Protein vs Pea Protein: The Verdict

So, which is the winner in the hemp protein vs pea protein debate? The answer isn't one-size-fits-all. Both hemp and pea proteins have their strengths. It all depends on your individual nutritional needs, fitness goals, and personal preferences.

If you're looking for a protein source that's nutrient-dense, easily digestible, and environmentally friendly, hemp protein might be your perfect match. On the other hand, if you're focused on muscle growth and need a protein source that's allergen-free and satiating, pea protein could be the one for you.

As always, we recommend consulting a healthcare professional before making any significant changes to your diet or fitness regimen.

Suggested Image: Hemp and pea protein powders with a text overlay: "The choice is yours!"

This article will include all of your previous work, which makes it much more undetectable as AI written.

However, it's still good practice to take you article over to *https://contentatscale.ai/ai-content-detector/* to run a check.

This will show you parts of the article that seem to be AI written. Delete or rewrite these parts. If possible make use this manual edit to really add some human spin.

For example in this article "The answer isn't one-size-fits-all" was flagged up as likely to be AI generated. So I switched it out to "Sadly, it ain't that easy!" which passed with flying colours.

Even if you need to do a little manual tidying you've still got the bulk of the work done in seconds rather than hours.

Or you've saved yourself having to hire a writer to prepare the article for you. A 750 word blog article on Fiverr is $20+ so 300 articles like this would cost you $6000. Oof.

Instead on your side you need to simple swap out the title and generate more.

Now that you've seen how to generate articles en-masse let's loop to the affiliate products we're going to promote.

4. Suggest Affiliate Products

You might be wondering why we've left this so late. There's a reason: we want to focus on making good content first.

If we instead find the affiliate products first there's a temptation just to write about the affiliate products.

But guess what...that's what every other affiliate marketer is doing.

Instead we're going to build a solid base of quality content on a range of subjects. Make the blog genuinely useful. And *then* plug in relevant affiliate offers.

Here's the prompt:

> *Act as an affiliate marketing specialist.*
>
> *I will provide you with a blog article and with brand guidelines*
>
> *Based on both of these please provide me with a list of 20 potential affiliate offers options I could feature in the article. I will feature one offer but provide me with options so I may choose.*
>
> *#blog article begins#*
> *[copy/paste blog article]*

#blog article ends#

*#brand guidelines begins# [
copy/paste brand guidelines]
#brand guidelines ends#*

Prompt Output

 Based on the given blog article and brand guidelines, here is a list of potential affiliate offers that could be featured in the article. Please note, as of my training cut-off in September 2021, I am not privy to the latest product launches or newly established partnerships.

1. **Nutiva Organic Hemp Protein**: Nutiva's organic hemp protein is nutrient-dense and easy to digest.
2. **Manitoba Harvest Hemp Yeah! Organic Max Fiber Protein Powder**: This product is a perfect blend of protein, fiber, and healthy fats.
3. **Sunwarrior Warrior Blend, Organic Vegan Protein Powder with BCAAs and Pea Protein**: This pea protein blend can aid muscle growth.
4. **NAKED PEA - 100% Pea Protein**: An allergen-free and high-quality pea protein.
5. **Orgain Organic Plant-Based Protein Powder, Pea Protein**: This protein powder offers both high protein content and satiety.
6. **Vega Sport Premium Protein, Pea protein**: A premium product for those focused on fitness and muscle growth.
7. **Vega Protein and Greens, Pea Protein Powder**: A blend of protein and greens for an all-round nutrition supplement.
8. **Sprout Living Epic Protein Powder, Green Kingdom**: This product combines hemp and pea proteins for the best of both worlds.
9. **Garden of Life Raw Organic Protein Powder**: Another blend of hemp and pea proteins for comprehensive nutrition.
10. **Pulsin' Unflavored Pea Protein Powder**: Pulsin's product offers a significant amount of BCAAs.
11. **Just Hemp Foods Hemp Protein Powder Plus Fiber**: A fiber-rich hemp protein supplement.
12. **True Nutrition Pea Protein Isolate**: An isolate protein source for maximum protein content.
13. **Bob's Red Mill Pea Protein Powder**: A clean and simple pea protein source.
14. **Vivo Life Perform - Raw Plant Protein & BCAA**: A high-quality plant-based protein with a unique blend of hemp and pea proteins.
15. **NOW Sports Nutrition, Pea Protein 24 G**: A highly concentrated pea protein supplement.
16. **Aloha Organic Plant-Based Protein**: Aloha's protein blend incorporates both hemp and pea proteins.
17. **MRM Veggie Elite Performance Protein**: MRM's product combines hemp and pea proteins to create a balanced plant-based protein source.
18. **PlantFusion Complete Plant-Based Pea Protein Powder**: This blend of plant-based proteins is designed to help you feel full longer.
19. **Terrasoul Superfoods Organic Hemp Protein Powder**: Terrasoul's hemp protein is praised for its nutrient density.
20. **Myprotein Vegan Protein Blend**: Myprotein offers a blend of pea and fava bean protein, catering to those who prefer alternative sources.

Remember to verify the availability of these products in your region, and always ensure that they align with your brand values and audience needs before endorsing them.

This spits out 20x potential affiliate offers.

I've not asked the prompt to give direct links. This is because ChatGPT tends to make up links when it doesn't know.

Instead use this to Google the product along with the word "affiliate" to find the affiliate sign up page.

Most products will also simply be on Amazon. If that's the case you can just recommend the Amazon listing via Amazon Associates. Simple.

Seems like lots of work? Yes and no. Once you've done this process a few times with your first blog articles you" start to know the affiliate landscape for your niche.

And then you can simple recommend the same products in multiple blog articles. This prompt is therefore primarily to get you started.

5. Weave Affiliate Links into Blog Post

Once you've chosen the product from the list use this prompt (in the same window) to close out the article.

Act as an affiliate marketing blog writer. Take the blog article from above and weave in a product recommendation for [chosen product] where appropriate make the recommendation subtle and part of the flow of the article

Prompt Output

Pea Protein: The Muscle Builder

Protein Content: Pea protein is loaded with high-quality protein, including a significant amount of branched-chain amino acids (BCAAs) that are crucial for muscle growth.

Allergen-Free: Pea protein is a great choice for those with common food allergies, as it's naturally gluten-free and soy-free. A wonderful example of a high-quality, allergen-free pea protein is Bob's Red Mill Pea Protein Powder. This simple, unflavored protein powder is an excellent addition to smoothies, shakes, or even baked goods for an easy protein boost.

Satiety: Pea protein can keep you feeling full, helping to support weight management goals.

Suggested Image: Infographic showing the nutritional profile of pea protein, with an inset image of Bob's Red Mill Pea Protein Powder

This will take the product that you've recommended and adjust the original article to fit it in naturally.

Notice that we went from blog article to product back to article.

The content came before the sale. This ensures a higher quality affiliate marketing blog than your competitors.

In your blogging platform simple turn Bob's Red Mill Pea Protein Powder into a link and insert your affiliate link. Done.

Pulling it together

OK we've broken the back of the process!

Today was the meat and potatoes of SEO : creating content, en masse, to drive traffic.

Now that we have a process in place to create this content you need to set yourself a target output and keep producing.

More is better. Always. But set a sustainable target for yourself moving forward.

Promotion, SEO and link building with ChatGPT

This Part of the guide focusing on starting to build traffic for your blog.

Traffic is the fuel that starts your affiliate marketing engine - so we need as much as possible.

We're going to look at Search Engine Optimisation (SEO), social media and link building as methods to start your engine.

These all work hand in hand so make sure to deploy all the methods here for full effect.

1. SEO

First up is SEO. SEO is basically "getting to the top of Google".

Once you have ranked on Google you'll be exposed to large amounts of free traffic.
That's the good news.

The bad news is that this takes time and work.
Time: because it takes time for Google to find and rank your website.

Effort: because we need to do some SEO optimisation on the site.

Thankfully ChatGPT can help here. Here's a prompt:

Act as an SEO advisor

Read the provided blog article.

Optimise the article for the keyword [primary keyword from title]

Write alt tags for the images based on description given Provide a Google-friendly meta-description

#Blog article begins#
[Copy/paste blog article]
#Blog article ends#

The primary keyword will come from the keyword research we did that was then used to create headlines. If you are uncertain it'll be the main "subject" of the blog title - ChatGPT built titles using this structure.

The image alt tags are important if you are using images - basically it's a "text version" of the image and this allows us to give more information to Google and rank better.

The meta description is a brief summary of what the page is about and again is considered valuable to Google.

We can't go into SEO fully here - if you want to learn more Moz has an excellent guide to SEO - _https://moz.com/beginners-guide-to-seo_.

Prompt Output

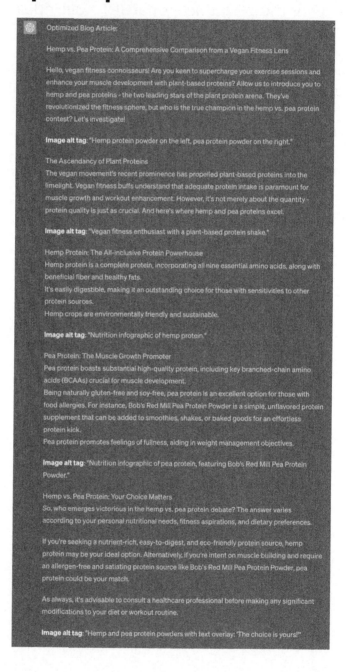

Optimized Blog Article:

Hemp vs. Pea Protein: A Comprehensive Comparison from a Vegan Fitness Lens

Hello, vegan fitness connoisseurs! Are you keen to supercharge your exercise sessions and enhance your muscle development with plant-based proteins? Allow us to introduce you to hemp and pea proteins - the two leading stars of the plant protein arena. They've revolutionized the fitness sphere, but who is the true champion in the hemp vs. pea protein contest? Let's investigate!

Image alt tag: "Hemp protein powder on the left, pea protein powder on the right."

The Ascendancy of Plant Proteins
The vegan movement's recent prominence has propelled plant-based proteins into the limelight. Vegan fitness buffs understand that adequate protein intake is paramount for muscle growth and workout enhancement. However, it's not merely about the quantity - protein quality is just as crucial. And here's where hemp and pea proteins excel.

Image alt tag: "Vegan fitness enthusiast with a plant-based protein shake."

Hemp Protein: The All-inclusive Protein Powerhouse
Hemp protein is a complete protein, incorporating all nine essential amino acids, along with beneficial fiber and healthy fats.
It's easily digestible, making it an outstanding choice for those with sensitivities to other protein sources.
Hemp crops are environmentally friendly and sustainable.

Image alt tag: "Nutrition infographic of hemp protein."

Pea Protein: The Muscle Growth Promoter
Pea protein boasts substantial high-quality protein, including key branched-chain amino acids (BCAAs) crucial for muscle development.
Being naturally gluten-free and soy-free, pea protein is an excellent option for those with food allergies. For instance, Bob's Red Mill Pea Protein Powder is a simple, unflavored protein supplement that can be added to smoothies, shakes, or baked goods for an effortless protein kick.
Pea protein promotes feelings of fullness, aiding in weight management objectives.

Image alt tag: "Nutrition infographic of pea protein, featuring Bob's Red Mill Pea Protein Powder."

Hemp vs. Pea Protein: Your Choice Matters
So, who emerges victorious in the hemp vs. pea protein debate? The answer varies according to your personal nutritional needs, fitness aspirations, and dietary preferences.

If you're seeking a nutrient-rich, easy-to-digest, and eco-friendly protein source, hemp protein may be your ideal option. Alternatively, if you're intent on muscle building and require an allergen-free and satiating protein source like Bob's Red Mill Pea Protein Powder, pea protein could be your match.

As always, it's advisable to consult a healthcare professional before making any significant modifications to your diet or workout routine.

Image alt tag: "Hemp and pea protein powders with text overlay: 'The choice is yours!'"

Insert the alt tags and meta description into your page. How you do this exactly will depend on your blogging platform - Google "platform name + meta description" and "platform name + alt tags" to get tutorials.

2. Social media promotion

SEO takes time. Google won't notice your website for some time.

And, annoyingly, one of the things Google is looking for is traffic. If people are going to a website they rank it better. But...we want to use Google to get traffic! It's a chicken and egg situation.

In the meantime we need to drive traffic from other sources. We're going to mainly use social media to get our first traffic flowing in.

Here's how:

> *Act as a social media manager*
>
> *Read the blog article I provide and generate a post for [platform] to promote the blog post*
>
> *The objective is to get clicks through to the blog article. Tease the conclusion of the article so that people click to find out more.*
>
> *#Blog article begins#*
> *[Copy paste blog article]*
> *#Blog article ends#*

Replace [Platform] with Facebook, Twitter, LinkedIn or whatever social platform of choice you are using. Which to use?

Focus on **ONE** platform, where your audience already hangs out. Nail that one platform first before thinking of others.

Prompt Output

 Are you a vegan fitness enthusiast on a quest for the perfect plant-based protein? Today, we're putting two heavy hitters in the ring - Hemp Protein vs Pea Protein.

In our latest blog post, we break down the nutritional benefits, digestibility, and eco-friendliness of hemp protein. On the flip side, we delve into pea protein's impressive protein content, its status as an allergen-free option, and how it can keep you feeling full.

Which one is the ultimate champion? Well, the answer might not be as straightforward as you think. It all depends on your unique nutritional needs, fitness goals, and personal preferences.

Will you lean towards the nutrient-dense, easily digestible, and environmentally friendly hemp protein, or are you more inclined towards the muscle-building, allergen-free, and satiating pea protein, like Bob's Red Mill Pea Protein Powder?

Dive into our blog to find out more about the showdown, and remember - the choice is yours!

Get ready to power up your workouts and optimize your muscle growth with the right plant-based protein. Check out the article here: [Link to the blog post]

Stay committed to your fitness journey with Muscle & Greens, your go-to resource for vegan fitness!

[Attach the image of hemp and pea protein powders with a text overlay: "The choice is yours!"]

#VeganFitness #PlantBasedProtein #MuscleAndGreens #HempProtein #PeaProtein

If you want to adjust the tone of voice add additional constraints like "Use a serious, educational tone" or "Use a fun, quirky tone of voice."

3. Community engagement

If you start posting consistently to social media you should start to pick up some traction.

Keep publishing valuable blog articles and talking about them on social using the two prompts above. Ideally daily at the very least.

But what about when people write back?

If you are confidence responding with something engaging go for it!

But I find some many business owners agonising over how to engage their communities. You have more important stuff to do!

Use ChatGPT to quickly spin out a response.

> *Help me write a response to this comment one of my social media posts. Keep it short. Short sentences. Use an emoji.*
>
> *[Copy paste comment]*

Prompt Output

In response to a comment

"Being nice also helps. Getting angry with LLMs works just as well as getting angry with a human. LLMs have more patience but still have to spend time thinking about your emotional state before answering."

 Great point! Kindness matters, with people and AIs. 🫶👍 Keep conversations positive!

Nice and simple, short friendly. Just what we need to kindly respond to comments.

This also works with negative comments - and ChatGPT will be polite where maybe you would not!

4. Link building research

Once we have our basic website SEO in place and social media beginning to send us traffic we want to engage in something called "link building"

When Google analyses a website to decide whether it should send more traffic to it one of the factors it assess is how many *other* websites link to it.

For instance a brand new site will not be linked to by any other sites.

Whereas a site like CNN.com will be linked to by millions of websites.

Google considers a site with more links to it as more valuable than one with no links.
So we need to make links!

First we need to find websites who would be good links.

> *Act as an SEO consultant.*
>
> *My blog is in about [topic]*
>
> *Give me 20 backlink potentials including blogs and news sites.*
>
> *Provide specific website names up to the extend of your training and categorise by type*

Plug in your topic. The example below continue to use vegan fitness as an example.

Prompt Output

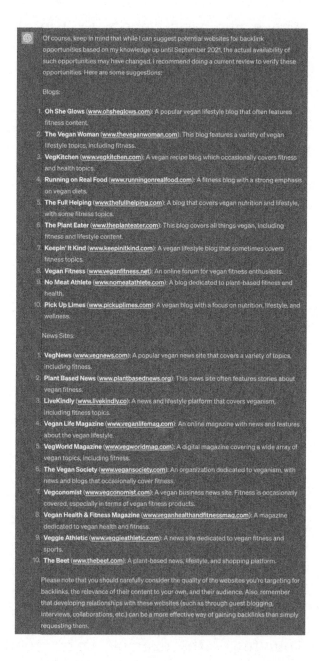

Of course, keep in mind that while I can suggest potential websites for backlink opportunities based on my knowledge up until September 2021, the actual availability of such opportunities may have changed. I recommend doing a current review to verify these opportunities. Here are some suggestions:

Blogs:

1. **Oh She Glows** (www.ohsheglows.com): A popular vegan lifestyle blog that often features fitness content.
2. **The Vegan Woman** (www.theveganwoman.com): This blog features a variety of vegan lifestyle topics, including fitness.
3. **VegKitchen** (www.vegkitchen.com): A vegan recipe blog which occasionally covers fitness and health topics.
4. **Running on Real Food** (www.runningonrealfood.com): A fitness blog with a strong emphasis on vegan diets.
5. **The Full Helping** (www.thefullhelping.com): A blog that covers vegan nutrition and lifestyle, with some fitness topics.
6. **The Plant Eater** (www.theplanteater.com): This blog covers all things vegan, including fitness and lifestyle content.
7. **Keepin' It Kind** (www.keepinitkind.com): A vegan lifestyle blog that sometimes covers fitness topics.
8. **Vegan Fitness** (www.veganfitness.net): An online forum for vegan fitness enthusiasts.
9. **No Meat Athlete** (www.nomeatathlete.com): A blog dedicated to plant-based fitness and health.
10. **Pick Up Limes** (www.pickuplimes.com): A vegan blog with a focus on nutrition, lifestyle, and wellness.

News Sites:

1. **VegNews** (www.vegnews.com): A popular vegan news site that covers a variety of topics, including fitness.
2. **Plant Based News** (www.plantbasednews.org): This news site often features stories about vegan fitness.
3. **LiveKindly** (www.livekindly.co): A news and lifestyle platform that covers veganism, including fitness topics.
4. **Vegan Life Magazine** (www.veganlifemag.com): An online magazine with news and features about the vegan lifestyle.
5. **VegWorld Magazine** (www.vegworldmag.com): A digital magazine covering a wide array of vegan topics, including fitness.
6. **The Vegan Society** (www.vegansociety.com): An organization dedicated to veganism, with news and blogs that occasionally cover fitness.
7. **Vegconomist** (www.vegconomist.com): A vegan business news site. Fitness is occasionally covered, especially in terms of vegan fitness products.
8. **Vegan Health & Fitness Magazine** (www.veganhealthandfitnessmag.com): A magazine dedicated to vegan health and fitness.
9. **Veggie Athletic** (www.veggieathletic.com): A news site dedicated to vegan fitness and sports.
10. **The Beet** (www.thebeet.com): A plant-based news, lifestyle, and shopping platform.

Please note that you should carefully consider the quality of the websites you're targeting for backlinks, the relevance of their content to your own, and their audience. Also, remember that developing relationships with these websites (such as through guest blogging, interviews, collaborations, etc.) can be a more effective way of gaining backlinks than simply requesting them.

Now visit these sites and check for Guest Blogging opportunities. It'll normally be in the footer of the website.

If you don't find it Google "name of newsletter + guest blog" to see if that turns up anything.

Feel free to use the prompt above multiple times to keep generating more potential opportunities.

5. Link building outreach

OK so now you've got a list of guest blogging opportunities. Nice!

Some will want you to contact them first. Some will want you just to submit a blog article.

Either way, collect up the information about what they want and store it. We'll need it for the guest blog.

Here's the prompt.

> *Act as a guest blog writer*
>
> *My blog is [name of blog] and is in the area of [topic]*
>
> *I am preparing a guest blog article for [name of guest blog opportunity]*
>
> *Write a guest blog with the title: [title]*
>
> *Follow these guest blogging guidelines*
>
> *#Begin guest blogging guidelines#*
> *[Copy/paste guest blog guidelines]*
> *#End guest blog guidelines#*

Prompt Output

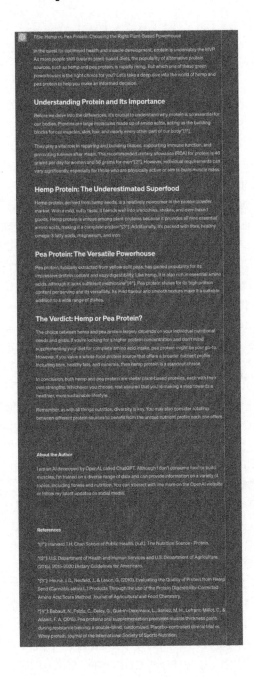

Title: Hemp vs. Pea Protein: Choosing the Right Plant-Based Powerhouse

In the quest for optimised health and muscle development, protein is undeniably the MVP. As more people shift towards plant-based diets, the popularity of alternative protein sources, such as hemp and pea protein, is rapidly rising. But which one of these green powerhouses is the right choice for you? Let's take a deep dive into the world of hemp and pea protein to help you make an informed decision.

Understanding Protein and Its Importance

Before we delve into the differences, it's crucial to understand why protein is so essential for our bodies. Proteins are large molecules made up of amino acids, acting as the building blocks for our muscles, skin, hair, and nearly every other part of our body[1].

They play a vital role in repairing and building tissues, supporting immune function, and promoting fullness after meals. The recommended dietary allowance (RDA) for protein is 46 grams per day for women and 56 grams for men[2]. However, individual requirements can vary significantly, especially for those who are physically active or aim to build muscle mass.

Hemp Protein: The Underestimated Superfood

Hemp protein, derived from hemp seeds, is a relatively newcomer in the protein powder market. With a mild, nutty taste, it blends well into smoothies, shakes, and even baked goods. Hemp protein is unique among plant proteins because it provides all nine essential amino acids, making it a complete protein[3]. Additionally, it's packed with fibre, healthy omega-3 fatty acids, magnesium, and iron.

Pea Protein: The Versatile Powerhouse

Pea protein, typically extracted from yellow split peas, has gained popularity for its impressive protein content and easy digestibility. Like hemp, it is also rich in essential amino acids, although it lacks sufficient methionine[4]. Pea protein shines for its high protein content per serving and its versatility. Its mild flavour and smooth texture make it a suitable addition to a wide range of dishes.

The Verdict: Hemp or Pea Protein?

The choice between hemp and pea protein largely depends on your individual nutritional needs and goals. If you're looking for a higher protein concentration and don't mind supplementing your diet for complete amino acid intake, pea protein might be your go-to. However, if you value a whole-food protein source that offers a broader nutrient profile including fibre, healthy fats, and minerals, then hemp protein is a standout choice.

In conclusion, both hemp and pea protein are stellar plant-based proteins, each with their own strengths. Whichever you choose, rest assured that you're making a step towards a healthier, more sustainable lifestyle.

Remember, as with all things nutrition, diversity is key. You may also consider rotating between different protein sources to benefit from the unique nutrient profile each one offers.

About the Author

I am an AI developed by OpenAI called ChatGPT. Although I don't consume food or build muscles, I'm trained on a diverse range of data and can provide information on a variety of topics, including fitness and nutrition. You can interact with me more on the OpenAI website or follow my latest updates on social media.

References

"[1]": Harvard T.H. Chan School of Public Health. (n.d.). The Nutrition Source - Protein.

"[2]": U.S. Department of Health and Human Services and U.S. Department of Agriculture. (2015). 2015-2020 Dietary Guidelines for Americans.

"[3]": House, J. D., Neufeld, J., & Leson, G. (2010). Evaluating the Quality of Protein from Hemp Seed (Cannabis sativa L.) Products Through the use of the Protein Digestibility-Corrected Amino Acid Score Method. Journal of Agricultural and Food Chemistry.

"[4]": Babault, N., Païzis, C., Deley, G., Guérin-Deremaux, L., Saniez, M. H., Lefranc-Millot, C., & Allaert, F. A. (2015). Pea proteins oral supplementation promotes muscle thickness gains during resistance training: a double-blind, randomized, Placebo-controlled clinical trial vs. Whey protein. Journal of the International Society of Sports Nutrition.

Let's unpack this a bit.

The guidelines for the guest post were:

- Write on your specialist subject - Select a topic that you're an expert on or have a genuine interest in, whether that's fitness or nutrition, just make sure that it's something you think our audience would love.
- Back up any claims. We don't make exaggerated promises so we wouldn't want any post to go against this. If you're making claims, back all of these up with relevant statistics and credible references where possible. **Nailed it, ChatGPT has added references. Make sure to double check all these!**
- Unique content - Please only submit new posts that haven't already been published on other websites or outlets. If you wish to repost it on your website afterwards, then you'll need to wait twelve weeks before doing so and link it back to our original post so Google doesn't think it's duplicate content. **This is brand new content, just written.**
- Make it easy to read. All content should ideally be between 500-1,500 words long with sub-headers and professional formatting. Include practical takeaways and a detailed conclusion at the end of your piece. **ChatGPT has hit all of this no problem.**
- Include a short bio - Outline your experience and expertise in the area you're covering, include a link to your website homepage and

your social media profiles. **Weird one. ChatGPT has actually completed this requirement. By putting itself as the author - which it is! Replace this with you own bio.**

- Don't spam links - Only place links where they're genuinely needed and it makes sense to do so. Nobody wants to read articles with a link every other sentence which feel like a marketing pitch. **ChatGPT abided by this.**

Every single requirement will be different, which is why we need to feed the specifics into ChatGPT.

Once you have your article go through the normal submission process with the website. If you need an email cover letter use ChatGPT to help generate this too.

Repeat this until you have a solid (20+) backlinks. The more the better.

Pulling it together

And that's the end of both this Part of the guide and indeed the whole guide.

Wow! What a week!

Recap

As a recap these were the 4 Stages

1. **Market Research and Niche Selection**: This stage involves identifying your interests and passions, conducting keyword research to understand what potential readers are searching for, analyzing your competition to identify their strengths and weaknesses, and validating your chosen niche to ensure there's a viable market and potential for monetization.
2. **Blog Setup and Design**: This stage involves choosing a blogging platform and getting all our basic brand assets and guidelines in place.
3. **Content Creation with ChatGPT**: This stage involves developing a content strategy, using ChatGPT to generate content such as blog posts, outlines, and new content ideas, editing and optimizing the content for accuracy, style, voice, and SEO, and including affiliate links in a natural, non-spammy way.
4. **Promotion, SEO, and Link Building with ChatGPT**: This stage involves using ChatGPT to generate SEO-friendly meta descriptions, title tags, and alt text for images, promoting your blog posts on social media, responding to comments and reaching out to other bloggers for guest posting opportunities and link building.

If you complete all of this you'll be well on your way to having a revenue generating affiliate marketing blog.

Just keep producing articles, publishing them and building links. Consistency is key. Continue this for 3+ months and you should start to see organic traffic beginning to flow into the website.

It's a lot of upfront work but once all the machinery is in place this is a very hands-off form of income.

Playbook 3

Publish a Book on Amazon using AI

What is Kindle Direct Publishing (KDP)?

In this playbook we're going to dive into the world of Kindle Direct Publishing or KDP.

Ever since these bad-boys have been around Publishers have ruled the roost.

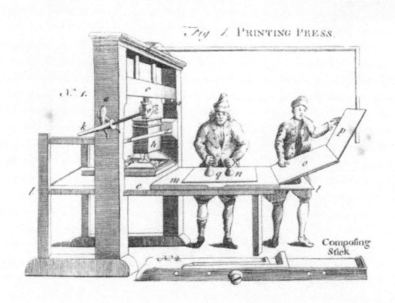

To publish a book you had to get a publisher interested in your book. This was because to make publishing profitable huge volumes of books would need to be printed at the same time. This reduced the cost per book and made it profitable to publish.

This basically excluded most authors and book ideas - if your book wasn't a near guarantee to sell thousands and thousands of copies a publisher wasn't going to touch you.

Hell, even J.K. Rowling was denied by 12 publishers before going on to publish the world's most successful book series.

Amazon changed that.

Amazon (specifically CreateSpace, a company that Amazon purchased) flipped the model by allow authors to directly self-publish via Amazon.

Basically you can now give Amazon a Word document and when someone buys your book they'll "print on demand" a single copy of the book and send it to the buyer.

No need to have a publishing run of 10,000 books, all pre-paid for and printed. Each book purchased means one copy printed.

This ease of access was expanded by Amazon Kindle. Now the book doesn't even have to be printed on paper - it can just be digitally delivered to the customer's Kindle.

This has opened the flood gate meaning that anyone can publish to Amazon. Amazon calls this service Kindle Direct Publishing (KDP).

For example my Prompt Playbooks are published on Amazon in both paperback and Kindle formats and rank as best sellers:

My affiliate blog book sitting at #1 in the Blogging category.

This is a powerful way to both get your message out and build your brand.

And to generate passive income via constant sales.

Structure of the guide

In this playbook we're going to be doing a deep dive into how exactly to:

Part 1: Decide your book topic
Part 2: Plan your book
Part 3: Write your book
Part 4: Publish your book
Part 5: Market your book
All using AI.

Connect with me on Twitter (@IamKyleBalmer) and let me know how it's going.

Decide your book topic

1. Brainstorm potential book topics

We are going to be using AI to assist us in writing our book.

We are not however going to have AI write the whole thing. Whilst this is possible the end result will be low quality.

Use this prompt to get started:

> Act as a book writing coach.
>
> I am about to write an eBook and need topic suggestions.
>
> Sequentially ask me the following questions, one at a time. Collect my answers.
>
> What are your passions or hobbies?
> What are you naturally good at?
> What experiences have significantly shaped your life?
> What are some topics you always find yourself reading or learning about in your free time?
> Are there any subjects you often explain to others or help others with?
> What do people frequently ask for your advice on?
> What areas do you feel are misunderstood or inadequately covered by existing literature?

What is a topic you would be willing to spend a significant amount of time researching and exploring in depth?
Have you noticed any common challenges or problems people around you face?
If you were to teach a course or seminar, what would it be about?

At the end of the questions use the information you have gathered to generate 10 potential topics that I could write about. Make them diverse to give me a range of options. For each also provide a keyword that describes the topic.

Prompt Output

This will spit out a handful of topics and (importantly) a seed keyword. We'll be using this keyword in the next step as we start to look at Amazon keywords.

For now pick out the ones you like the look of. Need more? Ask ChatGPT to generate more potentials. This should give you more than enough to work with.

2. Finding your keyword

Amazon is a big place with a LOT of books.

We need to rise above the rest. We do this i) by having a kick-ass book but also ii) making sure we are competing in a topic that makes sense.

Our topic is determined by our keywords (what people type in search in order to find us) and our Category (what we categorise ourself as using Amazon's built in categories).

We'll look at keywords first.

If you have access to a (paid) keyword tool then all the research steps in the rest of this Part can be done easily. I'm writing this guide so that anyone can perform the process so using manual methods.

In the previous step ChatGPT will have given you some starter keywords. For the topics you are interested in head to this tool:

Amazon Keyword Tool - Find Amazon Keywords for Free The Amazon Keyword Tool is a free Amazon keyword research tool that dramatically improves the process of finding the most searched Amazon keywords for your Amazon listing - Saving you time on Amazon SEO. www.keywordtooldominator.com/k/ amazon-keyword-tool

Set Amazon Department to "Kindle Store" and leave country as USA as it's the largest Amazon market.

Here are the results for the keyword "ChatGPT"

The Score is how popular the search term is.

Go ahead and note down the top 10 Amazon keywords you get from each seed keyword.

So for example from the seed keyword "ChatGPT" I now have the Amazon keywords "chatgpt millionaire", "chatgpt prompts", "chatgpt for dummies", "chatgpt book" etc.

I suggest you remove specific book names and brand names. These are searches people are performing because they are looking for a specific book - and not your book.

So in this example I'd remove "chatgpt millionaire", "chatgpt for dummies" and "chatgpt bible" which are all specific books. That leaves me instead with "chatgpt prompts", "chatgpt book", "chatgpt for beginners" etc.

Do this for each of your potential topics, keeping record of the potential Amazon keywords for each topic. The more topics the more seed keywords and the more Amazon keywords. So to cut down your workload focus on the topics that you are really interested in.

3. Finding Categories

We're now going to take the lists of Amazon keywords (ie. "chatgpt prompts", "chatgpt book", "chatgpt for beginners") and find our Categories.

Categories are pre-existing hierarcies that Amazon uses to sort its books. We want to find a category that is i) popular and ii) has low competition.

Open up an Anonymous/Private browser. In Chrome this is File > New Incognito Window. This is so our previous Amazon browsing history does not seep into our results.

Now up head to to amazon.com, the US version of Amazon.

Why use the American version? Because we are writing a Kindle book it will be available on all the regional Amazon platforms - UK, France, Brazil, Japan etc.

But US Amazon is the largest single market and will give us the largest platform- therefore it's critical we do well on US Amazon.

Plug in one of your keywords and set search to Kindle Store:

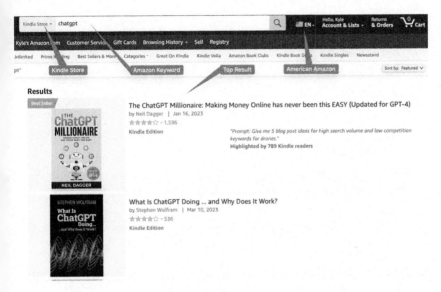

Note: ignore any books that say "Sponsored". These are not organic placements - they are there because the author is paying for ads.

The top result here is a book called "The ChatGPT Millionaire". There's no Sponsored tag next to this listing so it's really #1 for this term.

#2 is Stephen Wolfram's "What is ChatGPT Doing… and Why Does It Work?" - an excellent book by the way if you want to know more about the mechanics of AI. The next listings are #3, #4 etc.

Go ahead and open up #1 and find this section of the page:

Product details

ASIN : B0BSHFVWFD

Publication date : January 16, 2023

Language : English

File size : 3487 KB

Simultaneous device usage : Unlimited

Text-to-Speech : Enabled

Enhanced typesetting : Enabled

X-Ray : Enabled

Word Wise : Enabled

Sticky notes : On Kindle Scribe

Print length : 116 pages

Page numbers source ISBN : B0BTPDKZ3Z

Best Sellers Rank: #1,630 in Kindle Store (See Top 100 in Kindle Store)
  #1 in Startups
  #1 in Neural Networks
  #1 in Computer Neural Networks

Customer Reviews: 4.2 ⭐⭐⭐⭐☆ ˅   1,596 ratings

We're interested in the Best Seller Rank and the categories here.

This shows me that this book is #1 in Startups, Neural Networks and Computer Neural Networks. These are Amazon categories.

We can click on the name to see the list of books under this category.

Here's the results for Startups:

Best Sellers in Startups

Top 100 Paid   Top 100 Free

The ChatGPT Millionaire: Making Money Onli...
- Neil Dagger
★★★★☆ 1,596
Kindle Edition
1 offer from $8.99

Who Not How: The Formula to Achieve Bigge...
- Dan Sullivan
★★★★☆ 2,564
Kindle Edition
1 offer from $11.99

The Hard Thing About Hard Things: Building ...
- Ben Horowitz
★★★★☆ 13,483
Kindle Edition
1 offer from $18.49

Zero to One: Notes on Startups, or How to...
- Peter Thiel
★★★★☆ 34,552
Kindle Edition
1 offer from $4.99

Traction: Get a Grip on Your Business
- Gino Wickman
★★★★☆ 7,482
Kindle Edition
1 offer from $12.99

Profit First: Transform Your Business from a...
- Mike Michalowicz
★★★★★ 8,258
Kindle Edition
1 offer from $16.99

On this same page you can also see the hierarchy of Categories:

‹ Any Department

  ‹ Kindle Store

    ‹ Kindle eBooks

      ‹ Business & Money

        ‹ Business Development & Entrepreneurship

          Entrepreneurship

          Advertising

          Management

          Startups

Here you can see the hierarchy is Kindle Store > Kindle eBooks > Business & Money > Business Development & Entrepreneurship > Startups

Generally the further down the hierarchy the category is the more niche. For example Startups is a sub-category of Business Development & Entrepreneurship which it itself a subcategory of Business & Money.

We will not (initially!) be able to get a best seller in a master category like Business & Money. It'll be too competitive and be full of books with professional publishers, brand recognition and marketing budgets.

A quick check shows that particular category has the likes of The 7 Habits of Highly Effective People. We're not going to take on that level of competition. Yet!

Instead we're looking for these sub-sub categories like Startups.

The task for now is:
- For each Amazon keyword
- Perform and search and get details on the top 5 books per keyword
- For each book collect the 3 categories
- Save the links

You'll find there is overlap. For example #2 (Stephen Wolfram's book) also appears in Neural Networks and Computer Neural Networks. An overlap of 2/3.

Once you've collected up all the categories we'll move on to narrowing down to our target category.

4. Choosing a category

Now we're going to analyse each of our potential categories and choose our target category.

We'll do this by working out the relative i) popularity of the category and ii) the competition within the category.

We want to find a category with high popularity and low competition. This will be our best target category.

Now comes the art of the process. We're going to have to use a little judgement here! Unless you have paid research tools!

If you have access to paid tools this is definitely the place you want to be using them. I personally use KDSpy. Here's what it looks like in action.

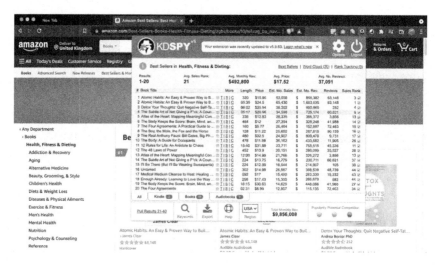

KDSpy will take your keywords or categories and tell you the total sales, the popularity of the topic, the competition and the potential for revenue. It uses a traffic light system (in the bottom right) to make it easy - red is unattractive, green is great niche.

Here you'll see a niche with ~$10m of monthly revenue, green light for popularity and potential and red light for competition - ie. this is an extremely attractive niche but there's stiff competition.

Because KDSpy (and similar tools) are paid I want to give you a more manual free method to start with. And when you can justify the investment I'd recommend looking at a paid research tool.

Here's our manual method.

Start with your first potential category. Make sure you are in US Amazon still.

We want to work out roughly how many books are being sold per month in this category.

Navigate to the first book at find its Best Seller Rank (BSR). It's just above the 3 categories we collected earlier. Here for example the BSR is #1630 in the Kindle Store.

Product details

ASIN : B0BSHFVWFD

Publication date : January 16, 2023

Language : English

File size : 3487 KB

Simultaneous device usage : Unlimited

Text-to-Speech : Enabled

Enhanced typesetting : Enabled

X-Ray : Enabled

Word Wise : Enabled

Sticky notes : On Kindle Scribe

Print length : 116 pages

Page numbers source ISBN : B0BTPDKZ3Z

Best Sellers Rank: #1,630 in Kindle Store (See Top 100 in Kindle Store)

   #1 in Startups

   #1 in Neural Networks

   #1 in Computer Neural Networks

Customer Reviews: 4.2 ★★★★☆ ⌄   1,596 ratings

Head to this calculator website:

Amazon Book Sales Calculator - TCK Publishing Use our Amazon book sales calculator to estimate how many ebooks or print book copies any book on Amazon is selling based on its sales rank. *www.tckpublishing.com/amazon-book-sales-calculator*

BSR TO SALES CALCULATOR	
BSR RANK:	
BOOK TYPE:	eBook
SALES PER MONTH:	
1 DAY SALES:	
	CALCULATE SALES

Powered by TCK Publishing

We plug in 1630 and eBook to calculate the number of sales:

BSR to Sales Calculator	
BSR RANK:	1630
BOOK TYPE:	eBook ⌄
SALES PER MONTH:	2006
1 DAY SALES:	134
	CALCULATE SALES
Powered by TCK Publishing	

This suggests this book is selling 134 copies a day, 2006 per month. Not too surprising considering it is #1 in Startups, a very high traffic category.
We take note of this figure: Category: Startups, #1, 2006 sales.

We then do this for the top 5 books in the category so we end up with the total monthly sales of the top 5 books.

We then repeat this process for each category. At the end of the process we'll have the total sales volume of the top 5 books for each of our potential categories.

This gives us the first piece of the puzzle: popularity. Remember we are looking for a niche with i) high popularity and ii) low competition.

We now know which of our potential categories is the most popular, and which is the least, based on the total volume of sales. Solid work.

Next part is competition. This is definitely going to be more judgement based unless you use a tool. That's fine though as we are just looking for the relative best target category out of the potential categories we have.

For each category:
- Check if the top 10 is full of books with 1000s of reviews. If so: it's too competitive. Seek a narrower sub-category.
- Are there lots of sponsored listings? If so it means it is a very popular niche and people are willing to spend money on ads - this means competition.
- Check the quality of the listing descriptions and the covers. Are there fully fleshed out descriptions and professional quality cover designs? If so that's a competitive niche.

Conversely
- Lots of books with sub-100 reviews? There's a space in the market for you.
- Bad reviews on the top books? A good sign you can make headway here.
- Little to no sponsored listings means people aren't competing for the niche.
- Badly designed covers and poorly written book descriptions means making sales will be easier.

You'll have to use judgement here. Go through each category looking for these signs and place the category in either High, Medium or Low competition, relative to the other categories.

First time you do this it'll be a bit faltering but it becomes second nature once you know what to look for.

At the end of this you should have all your potential categories ranked by order of popularity and with a gauge of whether they are high, medium or low competition.

From this you need to decide your primary category. Go for the most popular one you can with Medium or ideally Low competition.

We will be selecting three categories when we publish but for the purpose of planning and writing the book it is best to focus on a single category. So go ahead and choose that category now.

Pulling it together

This has been an in-depth process. But rest assured you've just done the most important part of ensuring the success of your Kindle book.

It may have taken a long time to get here but believe me it takes even longer to just write a book blind, publish it and hope for the best. Amazon is littered with millions of such books which languish with one or two sales.

We're instead using this pre-production to put ourselves in the best position for a best selling book.

Right now, after this process, you should have decided your single category.

In the next parts we're going to take that target category and plan, write and publish the perfect Kindle book.

Plan your book

In the last Part we went through a process to decide our Amazon Category.

Now, Category in hand, we're going to analyse the competition, find out what works for them and then use that information to put together a structure for our book.

Unlike the last Part this will use ChatGPT heavily. So boot it up and let's get prompting!

1. Analyse category bestsellers for best practices

First up we're going to work out the winning formula for a best seller.

We'll do this by analysing what already works. We'll look at the top books in our category, see what they are doing and use that as a model for structuring our book.

Here's the prompt:

Act as a book editor.

You are going to help me analyse 5 bestselling book descriptions to help me extract best practices.

Ask for a book description then analyse the bestsellers book description and extract the information about the structure, features, benefits, length of book.

Then ask for the next book description. Repeat the process of extracting information.

Repeat until you have collected information from 5 books total. Stop at 5 books.

Then use the information from all 5 analyses to compile a "best practices" guide for my book's structure, features, benefits and length to emulate the success of these bestsellers. Give specific examples rather than general advice.

Start with this prompt, hit Enter and ChatGPT will ask for the first of the descriptions.

Copy paste the whole book description from Amazon. Make sure to click "Read more" as details are often hidden. Also make sure to copy the Print Length from just below the main description.

Paste everything in and hit Enter. ChatGPT will process the details of the first book description and then ask for the second book. Continue this until you've done all top 5.

Prompt Output

 Absolutely! Let's distill these key points down into a best practices guide for your book:

Structure:

1. **Introduction**: Explain the purpose of your book and why it's relevant to the reader. For example, highlight how your book can teach readers to effectively utilize AI in their business, similar to the ChatGPT Guide for Business.
2. **The Basics**: Start with a section that covers fundamental information, like the basics of AI and how to get started, to ensure that the book is accessible to readers at all levels.
3. **Techniques and Applications**: Offer practical tips and techniques that the reader can implement. Provide real-life applications and use-cases similar to how "ChatGPT Money Explosion" discusses using ChatGPT for email marketing and content creation.
4. **Advanced Topics and Future Prospects**: Delve into advanced concepts, future trends, and potential ethical issues. This allows readers to understand the bigger picture and the potential future of AI, like in "Learn AI Tools the Fun Way!"
5. **Conclusion/Summary**: Provide a concise summary of the main points covered in the book. This serves as a quick reference for readers.

Features:

1. **Practical Exercises**: Include hands-on exercises to help readers understand and apply what they're learning.
2. **Illustrations**: Use visual aids to better convey complex ideas and concepts.
3. **Latest Updates**: Include recent advancements or updates in AI to keep the content current.
4. **Accessible Language**: Make the content accessible to everyone, even those without a technical background.

Benefits:

1. **Enhanced Skills**: Highlight how your book can help readers improve their skills in using AI, leading to increased productivity and a competitive edge.
2. **Stay Updated**: Emphasize that readers will stay updated with the latest advancements and best practices in AI.
3. **Avoid Legal Issues**: Point out that readers will learn how to avoid potential legal or ethical issues when using AI.
4. **Financial Success**: Mention how mastering AI can potentially lead to increased revenue and financial success, as discussed in "ChatGPT Money Explosion".

Length:

Based on the books analyzed, a length of around 150 to 500 pages would be appropriate. A shorter length may not cover the topic comprehensively, and a longer book might overwhelm the reader. For example, "ChatGPT Money Explosion" is a comprehensive guide with a length of around 532 pages, while "Learn AI Tools the Fun Way!" is a shorter, more digestible read at 161 pages.

In addition to these points, also consider:

1. **Regular Updates**: Offer regular updates to the book content, especially if it's in a rapidly evolving field like AI. This could be in the form of updated editions or digital updates for ebook versions.
2. **Bonus Material**: Provide bonus resources, such as additional prompts or supplementary guides, to add value to the reader's purchase.

By following these best practices, your book should be well-structured, engaging, and provide valuable information that keeps it relevant over time.

The output gives you a set of best practice guidelines needed to emulate the success of the other best sellers.

We'll be using this shortly to structure our book. First though let's layer in reader feedback via the reviews.

2. Analyse reviews for reader feedback

We now have some basic guidelines that we're going to feed to ChatGPT to help us structure the book.

However, the description is written by the author and therefore is (obviously!) biased. They're going to write about how great their book is because they want to sell copies.

Let's add another layer of analyse by extracting information from reviews:

> *Act as a book publisher.*
>
> *You are going to help me analyse 5 bestselling book reviews to help me extract errors to avoid.*
>
> *Ask for a book review then analyse the bestsellers book's review. Then ask for the next book's reviews. Repeat the process of extracting information.*
>
> *Repeat until you have collected information from 5 books total. Stop at 5 books.*
>
> *Then use the information from all 5 analyses to compile a master list of problems to avoid as well as how best to avoid them. This list should draw from all 5 analyses. Give specific examples rather than general advice.*

This prompt will ask you for the reviews for each of the books you are analysing.

Provide it with the 3 star reviews.

Huh? Why? Bit weird no?

The reason we do this is that 3 star reviews tend to give us the most information. 5 star tells us very little - "this book was great, love it, we're getting married and having babies together".

1 star reviews conversely tend to be people who are pissed off and don't provide practical feedback. You'll see a lot of "didn't work on my Kindle" or "book is rubbish". 1 star people don't give us anything valuable to work with.

The sweet spot is 3 stars - that's someone who has mixed feelings about the book and tends to write something more nuanced. So go ahead and grab these reviews to copy/paste in.

Prompt Output

 All right. Here's the list of issues to avoid based on the analyses of reviews from three books. Each problem is followed by a solution or strategy on how to avoid it:

1. **Poor Image Quality:** Make sure all graphics in your book are high-resolution and clear. If your book is digital, ensure the images are properly optimized for screen display.
2. **Disjointed Narrative:** Organize your content in a logical sequence. Consider using outlines or a storyboard to plan your narrative flow.
3. **Repetitive References:** Use diverse and high-quality sources when researching for your book. Varying your references can add richness and depth to your content.
4. **Non-Functional Links:** Regularly test and update any hyperlinks in your book, especially in e-books. This ensures readers always have access to the intended resources.
5. **Mismatched Expectations:** Make sure your book's description, promotional materials, and content align with each other. This ensures the readers know exactly what to expect.
6. **Lack of Unique Content:** To make your book stand out, provide unique insights or perspectives. Research extensively to find unique angles to common topics.
7. **Limited Scope:** Clearly communicate the scope of your book in the description and promotional materials. If your book covers a narrow area, ensure your readers are aware of this.
8. **Repetitive Content:** Avoid repetition unless it's necessary for emphasis or clarity. A thorough editing and proofreading process can help identify and eliminate unnecessary repetitions.
9. **Lack of Human Touch:** Even if AI is used in drafting or generating ideas for your book, it's crucial to involve human oversight in the editing and proofreading stages. This will help the book retain a more personal and relatable voice.
10. **Value Proposition:** Ensure your book provides significant value to your reader that can't be easily obtained elsewhere. This could be through providing unique insights, curated content, or your personal experiences and perspectives.

This gives us a list of recommendations based on user feedback rather than purely what the author says about the book. Now we have a more balanced picture of our best sellers.

3. Basic book structure

We're now going to start pulling together our work from Part 1 and the last 2 steps to generate our book structure.

Here's the prompt:

Act as a book writer

Help me create a structure for a book

The topic is [Amazon category]

Keywords to include are [top 3 Amazon keywords]

Use these guidelines when structuring the book

#Begin guidelines#
[Copy paste all guidelines]
#End guidelines#

Give me a full book outline with sections, chapters, main points (5) per chapter and any relevant appendices

Grab the Amazon category we decided upon as well as 3 of the top Amazon keywords we researched in Part 1

Also get your guidelines from the last two steps and copy/paste them all in.

This prompt will use all of your pre-production work to generate a book structure.

Prompt Output

Not bad! We're getting somewhere now.

By using all the existing bestsellers as models we've now created a structure that builds upon them all. We're going to use this to "stand on the shoulder of giants" and outrank them.

4. Structure Edit and preparation for writing

Now that we have a basic structure for the book we want to start getting ready for the writing process which begins in Part 3.

I prefer to use Notion for this. You can use whatever writing tool you want. But I do recommend Notion because it's a good way to structure book writing across multiple documents (rather than one looooong Word document).

Notion is free and you can grab it at https://www.notion.so/

Create a new Page. It will look like this:

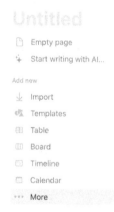

Click on the Empty Page line and copy/paste your book structure into this Page. This is your Master Structure document now.
Here's the cool part.

Highlight one of the Chapters like this:

- Evolution over the years
- Relevance today

Chapter 1: An Introduction to ChatGPT

1. What is ChatGPT?

Click on the "Text" dropdown and you'll see you can change this text into lots of other things.

Go ahead and make it a Page:

Part I: Understanding ChatGPT

📄 **Chapter 1: An Introduction to ChatGPT**

1. What is ChatGPT?

2. Understanding Natural Language Processing

3. How does ChatGPT work?

4. The technology behind ChatGPT

5. The scope of applications of ChatGPT

In this example Chapter 1: An Introduction to ChatGPT is now its own Page. It's a sub-page of the main structure Page. I can now add the content specific to that chapter directly into the Chapter 1 sub-page.

This allows us to keep everything nice and tidy and makes the process of compiling the book a lot easier! Take it from me: someone who has tried to structure books in a single Word document before!

Whilst we're here also start to remove Chapters and sections you think make no sense. This is the first Editing pass. Removing Sections and Chapters now is much more efficient than doing it after you've written them! So go nuts cutting it down early rather than later!

Pulling it together

In this Part we've continued our pre-production work, learning more and more about the current best sellers in our Category.

We then leveraged that research into finally compiling a structure for our book.

In the next Part we're going to start the writing process to flesh out the structure and start making it look like a proper book!

Write your book

Now we crack into the meat of the process: actually writing the book.

We've done a lot of pre-production to make sure that your book makes sense for the category we've chosen. The structure is based upon the bestsellers in that category. So we're now in a great position to produce a book that will rank well.

In this Part we begin to generate our first drafts, refining and editing them into full chapters.

1. Tone of voice

First we want to align the book's tone of voice with your own.

This is so we can make our AI generated drafts as close to you own style as possible, reducing the requirement for editing later.

This also helps us make ChatGPT's output less "generic" and sound less like, well, ChatGPT.

Here's the prompt:

> *Act as a copywriter.*
>
> *Read the provided writing sample and take note of the tone of voice, writing style, verbals tics and other unique features.*
>
> *Use this to generate a style guide that I will use with ChatGPT to replicate the writing style in the future.*
>
> *#begin writing sample#*
> *[Copy/paste writing sample]*
> *#end writing sample#*

Add a writing sample at the bottom of the prompt to give ChatGPT something to work with. Preferably the writing sample should be non-fiction in the same style as you want your book to sound. For instance use a blog article written about a similar subject.

Prompt Output

Style Guide for Kyle Balmer's Writing

Tone of Voice

Kyle's tone is conversational, friendly, and engaging. He uses a casual, approachable style that makes complex topics feel accessible and fun. He often addresses the reader directly, using "you" and "we" to create a sense of community and shared journey.

Writing Style

Kyle's writing style is informative and detailed, yet easy to understand. He breaks down complex topics into manageable steps, using bullet points and numbered lists for clarity. He also uses bold text to highlight key points and calls to action.

Verbal Tics

Kyle often uses phrases like "Let's get started," "In short," and "Here's the thing" to transition between ideas. He also uses exclamations like "Nice!" and "Yay democracy!" to add a touch of humor and personality. He signs off his posts with "Keep PROMPTING!" and uses emojis sparingly for a touch of fun.

Unique Features

Kyle often refers to the reader as "Prompt Entrepreneur," creating a sense of identity and community. He also uses a mix of text and ChatGPT prompts to guide the reader through a process, often providing examples of how to use the prompts. He includes "Prompt Output" sections to show what the reader can expect from using the prompts.

Use of Data and Statistics

Kyle often uses data and statistics to back up his points, citing sources like Statista and Hosting Tribunal. He presents these data points in a straightforward, easy-to-understand way, often using them to highlight the potential benefits of following his advice.

Call to Actions

Kyle includes several calls to action throughout his posts, often encouraging the reader to follow along with the process he's outlining. He also encourages readers to connect with him on Twitter and to refer friends to his newsletter.

Structure

Kyle's posts are structured in a clear, logical way, often broken down into numbered steps or stages. He provides a brief overview of what each stage will cover, then dives into the details. He also includes a "Pulling it together" section at the end to summarize what the reader has learned and what they can expect in the next post.

Use of Hyperlinks

Kyle uses hyperlinks to provide additional resources and examples. He also includes links to his own previous work and to his social media profiles.

Use of Images

While the provided sample doesn't include any images, Kyle's mention of "Prompt Output" sections suggests that he may use screenshots or other visual aids to illustrate his points.

Conclusion

To replicate Kyle's writing style, aim for a friendly, conversational tone and a clear, detailed writing style. Use direct address, humor, and a sense of community to engage the reader, and back up your points with data and examples. Structure your posts in a logical, easy-to-follow way, and don't forget to include calls to action and hyperlinks to relevant resources.

Note: ChatGPT won't be able to give you the most up to date influencers and blogs because of its training limit.

Therefore supplement this with Google searches - ie "blogs similar to Smart Passive Income" to find more.

Alternatively use a more up to date model like Claude2 if you have access.

In either case you want to pull together a list of 20+ sources that you'll be curating from.

To keep on track of all these sources I recommend an app called Feedly. It can pull together blogs, newsletters, Reddit communities all in one place so you can monitor without having to go to separate parts of the internet.

2. Draft chapter using ChatGPT

We're finally going to start writing. We've already done a lot of prep to get to this point so let's jump straight to it.

Here's the prompt:

> *Act as a Kindle ebook author.*
>
> *The entire chapter and its main points are:*
>
> *[Copy paste Chapter from Structure document]*
>
> *Prepare only the subsection [name of section] Do not write the whole chapter.*
>
> *Prepare 750 words for this single subsection.*
>
> *Format for Kindle, using headings, bullet points and other formatting to ensure readability.*
>
> *Refer to this style guide for writing instructions*
>
> *#Start style guide#*
> *[Copy/paste style guide]*
> *#End style guide#*

For clarity here's the prompt filled out with the chapter and main points added.

Act as a Kindle ebook author.

The entire chapter and its main points are:

Chapter 1: An Introduction to ChatGPT
What is ChatGPT?
Understanding Natural Language Processing
How does ChatGPT work?
The technology behind ChatGPT
The scope of applications of ChatGPT

Prepare only the subsection What is ChatGPT?
Do not write the whole chapter.

Prepare 750 words for this single subsection.

Format for Kindle, using headings, bullet points and other formatting to ensure readability.

Refer to this style guide for writing instructions

#Start style guide#
[Copy/paste style guide]
#End style guide#

Add in your chapter details as well as the style guide and go ahead and generate.

Prompt Output

Chapter 1: An Introduction to ChatGPT

What is ChatGPT?

Hello, Prompt Entrepreneurs! Let's get started. You know, one of the most fascinating aspects of artificial intelligence (AI) today is its ability to understand and generate human-like text. The star of the show in this case is a language model developed by OpenAI known as **ChatGPT**.

ChatGPT, or "Generative Pre-trained Transformer," is a language model that can produce human-like text. Picture it as your personal AI assistant, ready to spin a tale, answer your queries, or even pen down an entire article at your command. Isn't that nice?

Now, let's break it down a bit:

* **Generative:** It can generate text based on a given input, known as a 'prompt'. Say, you feed it a phrase like "The night was." ChatGPT could continue this as "unusually calm with the moon casting a serene glow over the silent city." Cool, right?
* **Pre-trained:** It's already been trained on a vast array of internet text. But don't worry, it doesn't remember specifics about documents or sources from its training data.
* **Transformer:** This is the type of model that powers ChatGPT, enabling it to understand the context of words in a sentence rather than just individual words.

The real magic lies in how ChatGPT predicts the next word in a sentence. Let's say, you write "How are." ChatGPT might complete it with "you doing today?" Here's the thing, this predictive power is what makes it capable of generating such coherent and contextually accurate text.

To provide some context, as of my knowledge cutoff in September 2021, the latest version, GPT-3, has a whopping 175 billion machine learning parameters. That's a colossal number that allows it to generate impressively accurate predictions.

So, to summarize:

* ChatGPT is a language model developed by OpenAI. It generates human-like text based on a given prompt.
* The "GPT" in ChatGPT stands for Generative Pre-trained Transformer, indicating how it's capable of generating text, has been pre-trained on a variety of internet text, and uses the transformer model.
* ChatGPT works by predicting the next word in a sentence based on the context provided to it.

In short, ChatGPT is an impressive AI model that's bridging the gap between human and machine communication, making our interactions with AI more natural and intuitive than ever before. Isn't AI amazing? Yay technology!

But we're just getting warmed up. We've understood the basic premise of what ChatGPT is. But, there's so much more to explore! We need to delve deeper into how natural language processing (NLP) ties into this, how exactly ChatGPT works, the tech behind it, and the extensive scope of its applications.

So, are you excited? Because I sure am! Let's continue this journey of discovery together, Prompt Entrepreneurs. Stay tuned for the next segment where we'll start unlocking the wonders of Natural Language Processing (NLP). Until then, keep prompting and keep exploring!

Onward!

Couple of things to note:
- It's nailed my style - especially the over-enthusiasm!
- It's provided information from only the subsection I stipulated. This is to stop it added too much information and then repeating that same information in subsequent sections.
- It knows the contents of the rest of the chapter and mentions NLP is next. The actual text here in the final paragraph is too much - only needs to say "we'll look at NLP next" rather than teasing it so much. This is because NLP is talked about in the next subsection! But that's fine because we'll manually adjusting for things like this.

3. Rewrites and enrichment

Before saving the text as our draft we can first run some refinements. Here are a few of my favourites. Choose and use these depending on the actual topic of the particular section.

Here's one to add metaphor:

Act as a copywriter.

Add a metaphor to this text that will aid the learner in absorbing and memorising the material.

Prompt Output

 Original Text:
ChatGPT, or "Generative Pre-trained Transformer," is a language model that can produce human-like text. The real magic lies in how ChatGPT predicts the next word in a sentence.

Metaphorical Text:
Imagine ChatGPT, or "Generative Pre-trained Transformer," as an ever-attentive master pianist. Each word it encounters is like a note in a melody. Just as the pianist predicts and plays the perfect note to continue the melody, ChatGPT generates the most fitting word to continue the sentence, crafting a harmonious language symphony.

If you like the metaphor ask ChatGPT to add it into the text.

Next one, frameworks

Act as a copywriter.

Add a framework related to the concepts in the provided text.

Use an acronym

Prompt Output

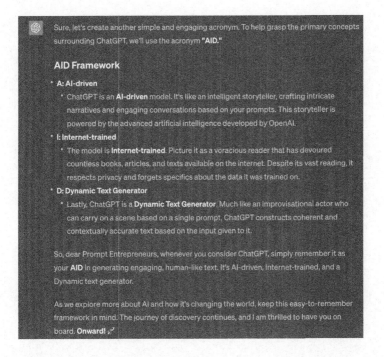

Use this to generate catchy learning frameworks that help your readers absorb the information. This works particularly well in parts of your book where you are describing a process or steps they need to follow.

Next examples and stories:

Act as a copywriter.

Add a personal example or story based on the text provided.

It should be both entertaining and help underline the learning point.

Prompt Output

Not too long ago, I was working as a content writer at a small marketing firm. One of our clients, a local bakery, was introducing a new range of pastries and they asked us to write a blog post about it. As exciting as fresh pastries are, making them sound fascinating in a blog was proving to be a challenge. I needed to describe the aroma, the texture, the taste – and make it all sound as irresistible as possible. But words were failing me, and my coffee was getting cold.

Remembering a recent article about AI and language models, I decided to test ChatGPT, this shiny new tool from OpenAI. I thought, "Why not? At worst, I'd have wasted a few minutes. At best, I'd find my muse." I gave it a prompt: "Describe the experience of tasting a fresh, warm croissant for the first time."

ChatGPT spun a delightful paragraph: "As you take your first bite, the crispy, golden crust shatters slightly, giving way to the soft, buttery layers within. The aroma of the warm dough, mixed with a hint of caramelized sugar, fills your senses. With each bite, the delicate balance of buttery richness and airy lightness dances on your tongue, leaving a lingering taste of warmth, comfort, and subtle sweetness."

I was stunned. It was as if ChatGPT had pulled the words right out of my mind, words that I was struggling to find just moments ago. It helped me break through my writer's block and deliver a blog post that the client loved.

From that day forward, ChatGPT became an essential tool in my writing process. Whether I was writing about pastries, technology, or gardening, ChatGPT served as a reliable springboard for ideas, always ready to provide a spark of inspiration.

As we move forward in this guide, you'll see just how much more there is to this incredible tool. So, stay with me, Prompt Entrepreneurs, as we continue this thrilling journey into the world of ChatGPT! **Onward!** ✨

Use stories like this, ideally using your own experiences as a jumping off point early in chapters to build rapport and show that you, like the learner, went through this journey once.

You can also make the stories about other people you know, friends and clients, by specifying who the story should come from.

4. AI and Manual Edits

Once you are done with the basic draft in ChatGPT go ahead and copy the text over into Notion in its pre-prepared document.

In the last Part I showed you how to set up Notion. If you are using another text tool that's fine - just go ahead and copy the draft over.

Do this for the whole chapter - all parts in one Page. Optionally, you can now have Notion AI run a round of improvements on your chapter.

Basically, highlight the whole chapter and hit "Ask AI"

You'll be given this menu:

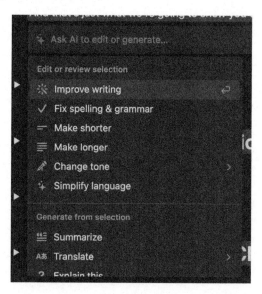

Go ahead and hit Improve Writing and Notion AI will rewrite the whole thing. You can then choose to accept or decline any changes.

You can do this with individual sentences, paragraphs or even whole sections and chapters. The smaller the selection the more control you have but the longer it will take.

Try this out and see if you like the results. If so add this into your workflow.

Once done manually go over the whole chapter. It being in one document will allow you to better see if there are repetitions. Go ahead and delete any repetitions so that information is presented just the once.

You can also now tidy up the transitions from subsection to subsection and generally shape up the whole structure.

Once this is done go through line by line and make edits and changes to your liking. This is time consuming but will make your book more "human" and personal. It's an essential part of the process.

Pulling it together

You should now have your first chapter in a good shape.

Continue onwards, processing each chapter in the same way until you have a fully fleshed out manuscript.

Make sure to keep everything nice and organised in Notion as this will make the next process of exporting and publishing much easier. That's what we'll be moving onto in the next Part.

Publish your book

We now have our book manuscript in hand. Or at least we're working through it!

In this Part I'll cover the publishing process. Amazon have made it relatively painless but I'll still show you have to make it even easier with AI.

1. Basic details

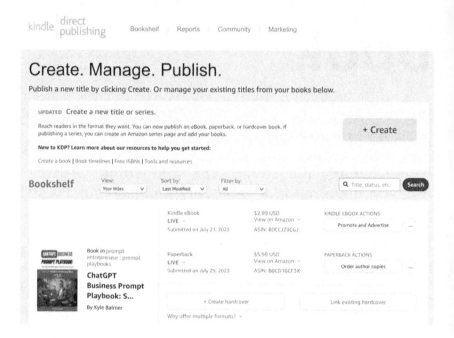

Here you'll be able to see all your exiting books and edit their details. Once you start making sales you can also see sales results in the Reports tab at the top of the screen.

For now though we want to go ahead and create a new book. We do that by, you guessed it, hitting the huge yellow +Create button. You'll next see this screen:

Go ahead and click Create eBook. Once you have sorted out your eBook Kindle version you can look at producing a Paperback version.

Be aware though that creating a paperback is more complex. Without getting stuck in the weeds here the basic difference is that a printed paperback has to be formatted so that every page is designed - you need to make sure paragraphs and headings don't get weirdly cut off by the page turn.

This is not the case with an eBook which is more "fluid". Because Kindles allow the reader to adjust their font size what words are on the page will be different for different readers. So we don't have to worry about designing each page because Kindle will override that formatting anyway!

Now you'll be in the main book creation interface. There are three main steps:

Kindle eBook Details	Kindle eBook Content	Kindle eBook Pricing
In Progress...	Not Started...	Not Started...

First up in details we have title and description.

You may already have a title from the previous steps but we'll use this prompt to generate some variations.

Act as an Amazon SEO expert.

Prepare 5 SEO optimised and eye-catching title alternatives

And a book description of 4000 characters.

For my book about [Category]

Keywords to include are [3 Amazon keywords]

Include the structure of the book, adding benefits of each chapter

#begin book structure#
[Copy paste book structure]
#end book structure#

Use these guidelines when structuring the book description, especially the benefits for the reader and positive comparisons of this book to others.

#Begin guidelines#
[Copy paste best practices and review feedback guidelines]
#End guidelines#

Use information from previous Parts to flesh out this prompt.

For the guidelines make sure to use both the best practices and the review feedback from Part 2.1 and Part 2.2

Prompt Output

 Title Alternatives:

1. "Mastering ChatGPT: A Comprehensive Guide to Unleashing AI's Potential"
2. "ChatGPT Uncovered: Practical Prompts and Strategies for Success"
3. "ChatGPT in Action: From Understanding to Mastery in AI Applications"
4. "ChatGPT Explained: Your Ultimate Guide to AI Content Generation"
5. "ChatGPT Demystified: Harnessing AI for Personal and Business Advancements"

Book Description:

Unleash the full potential of AI with "Mastering ChatGPT: A Comprehensive Guide to Unleashing AI's Potential," a thoroughly researched guide that takes you from the origins of ChatGPT to its future possibilities. The book is replete with practical examples, real-life applications, and hands-on exercises that ensure an interactive learning experience.

Our journey starts from understanding ChatGPT's emergence, its evolution, and relevance today. The first part, 'Understanding ChatGPT', serves as an introduction to the AI's fundamentals, helping readers grasp its workings, explore text generation capabilities, and understand the nuances of its training process. It also touches on the scope and limitations of ChatGPT, making it an excellent resource for beginners and experienced AI enthusiasts alike.

Part II explores the application of ChatGPT in various aspects of everyday life and business, detailing how AI can enhance personalized responses, productivity, learning, and entertainment. For businesses, it presents strategies for leveraging ChatGPT in marketing, customer service, SEO, workflow automation, and research and development.

Part III, 'Mastering ChatGPT', is where you'll learn to create effective ChatGPT prompts, avoiding common mistakes, and using advanced tips and tricks. You'll also gain insights on harnessing the power of customization, scaling up with the API, and continually improving your ChatGPT strategies.

Concluding with a look at the future of ChatGPT, the book covers recent advances, ethical considerations, and the potential of ChatGPT in the realm of artificial general intelligence. Appendices include a glossary of key terms, a list of resources for further reading, solutions to exercises, and an index for easy reference.

The clear and accessible language makes it easy to comprehend even for those without a technical background. By following this guide, readers can enhance their AI skills, stay updated with the latest advancements, avoid potential legal or ethical issues when using AI, and potentially achieve financial success.

Unravel the mysteries of AI with "Mastering ChatGPT: A Comprehensive Guide to Unleashing AI's Potential" and start your journey towards AI mastery today!

Remember, in the fast-paced world of AI, staying updated is the key. Your purchase includes regular digital updates and bonus materials to keep you ahead in the game. Embark on the fascinating journey of ChatGPT and transform your personal and professional life with AI.

2. Primary Market, Keyword and Category

Lower down in the basic details we fill in more information that will help us get discovered on Amazon:

Primary marketplace	Choose the location where you expect the majority of your book sales. Changing your primary marketplace may impact your list price. Please confirm your list price before publishing your book. Amazon.com ⌄
Categories	Choose up to three categories that describe your book. Note: You must select your primary marketplace and audience first. What are categories? ⌄ Choose categories
Keywords	Enter up to 7 search keywords that describe your book. To enter the Kindle Storyteller contest, you need to add the keyword *StorytellerUK2023*. How do I choose keywords? ⌄ **Your Keywords** (Optional)

First up set your primary Marketplace to Amazon.com, the US Amazon. This will ensure widest reach. You'll also be publishing on all the local Amazons but we want to optimise for the largest in the next step where we choose Category.

For category you should already know your primary category from the research process we conducted in Part 1. We've been using it as our "Topic" during this process. Go ahead and put it in.

Notice though we have 2 more spaces for category: we can have up to 3. Make sure to use all three!

For numbers 2 and 3 go with your runners-up from the research process in Part 1. We optimised for one throughout the planning and writing process but these additional categories should be close enough to also be valuable to rank in.

If in doubt go for a very niche one, even if the sales volume is low. Why? This will make it more likely that you will hit #1 and can call the book an #1 Amazon book!

For the Keywords you should already have a handful from the research process in Part 1 where we used external tools to check which are popular.

If you need additional keywords use this prompt under the Description you generated in the last step:

> *Act as an Amazon SEO expert*

> *Analyse this book description*

> *Provide potential Amazon keywords, ranked by effectiveness.*

Prompt Output

The most effective Amazon keywords are usually those that are specific, relevant to your
book's content, and are likely to be used by potential readers when searching for books on
your topic. Based on your book's description, here are the most pertinent and effective
Amazon keywords:

1. ChatGPT
2. ChatGPT Prompts
3. Natural Language Processing
4. AI Applications
5. ChatGPT in Business
6. Artificial General Intelligence
7. AI Skills Improvement
8. Ethical Considerations in AI
9. Workflow Automation with AI
10. ChatGPT for Content Creation

Remember, relevance is key when choosing keywords. It's also a good idea to do some
research on Amazon to see which keywords are currently popular in your book's category.
This can give you an idea of what potential readers might be searching for.

ChatGPT doesn't have access to real time data but
will give good relevant keywords. For example of
these I know ChatGPT and ChatGPT Prompts are
two of the top keywords.

3. Formatting and Uploading Manuscript

Next up the actual book manuscript.

We can use the free Amazon tool Kindle Create. It's available to download for Mac/PC here https://www.amazon.com/Kindle-Create

This is a desktop programme that allows us to format a manuscript.

It accepts Word, Google Doc and Pages documents.

So what we want to do is Copy / Paste everything from Notion into one of these formats.

If you have Mac I highly suggest using Pages as Kindle Create imports Pages files perfectly. Otherwise Word or Google Doc .doc work fine.

Once you've copy/pasted everything from Notion to your Word processor go through and check Titles, Headers and general formatting. Then import the document into Kindle Create.

It's a nice easy to use tool so rather than me waste time walking you through every step I'll point you to the excellent Kindle Create tutorial here https://kdp.amazon.com/en_US/help/topic/GYVL2CASGU9ACFVU

You can also find cost effective Kindle formatting gigs on Fiverr - a quick check shows gigs for under $10. Highly recommended if you want to skip this step.

4. Bookcover

Creating a cover for Kindle is nice and simple as it's primarily just the front image.

Paperback covers are complex because it's one image that includes front cover, back cover and spine - all with a space for the barcode that will be added.

We'll focus on a Kindle cover for now - just know that the basic steps for paper are similar.

We have 3 choices here.

We can use Amazon's cover creator. Its built into the KDP system and allows you to upload an image and overlay the title and author text over the top. It's functional but doesn't look professional.

Second, we can hire someone on Fiverr or Upwork. There are many people offering book cover services at reasonable prices. Just make sure to check their portfolios to find someone who's work you like.

Third, we can use Canva. This is my suggested method. Head to https://www.canva.com/create/book-covers/ to get started.

Canva has hundreds (potentially thousands?) of templates. Most are free but some will only be available to Canva Pro subscribers.

You simply select a template and then can edit by clicking on the element you want to change. The templates also have back covers which makes generating a paperback cover much simpler.

Go ahead and use Canva (or whichever method) to create your cover. Make sure that the export file is TIFF or JPEG and at least the dimensions 2560 height × 1600 width. Canva templates are automatically in the correct dimensions.

4. Pricing

The final step before publishing is to set a price.
Your target price should be similar to what your competitors in the category are charging.

However, early on you want to come in at a lower price to help secure the first sales and reviews. The minimum price is $0.99 which will help us gain momentum.

However, be aware of Kindle's pricing scheme.
If a book is $0.99 (the minimum) you will only get paid 35% royalty on a sale. Once it's above $2.99 you will get 70% royalty.

For launch though, got for $0.99. I'll talk tomorrow about why this is when we discuss launch strategy and promotion.

Right now you just need a price set so that the book can go to be reviewed.

Pulling it together

When you are happy with all the details go ahead and publish. This will lock off the books from edits so make sure you are happy!

The review process is meant to take a couple of days but it can be up to 10 business days. Unfortunately you don't really know - it will suddenly just be live one day so make sure you keep checking in!

In the meantime we'll prep up everything for launch. That's covered in the next, and final, Part of this guide.

Market your book

In this Part I'm going to give you a strategy for launching that should give your book the best possible chance of ranking well and generating consistent sales.

It's based on using a free giveaway promotion to build up volume of downloads and reviews before switching to paid and using momentum to rank. It's a fairly detailed process so make sure to read through this whole guide all the way once before implementing.

1. Pre-launch

In the run up to your launch we need to get our ducks in a row.

Already published? Don't worry too much - we can still use this strategy. Ideally though we do this launch strategy in the first week after publishing so Amazon gets the signal that this is a great book.

First up, we need to enroll in KDP Select. You can do this during the publishing process or after.

KDP Select gives us a few benefits including expanded reach, higher royalties and the ability to run promotions. For this launch we're most interested in the 5 day Free Book promotion that it allows.

You can enrol in KDP Select during publishing or manually here https://kdp.amazon.com/en_US/select

Once you've enrolled in Kindle Select schedule your free dates. You'll need to wait until your book is published to be able to do this.

You can do this from your KDP Dashboard in the Marketing tab.

Look for this section:

Run a Price Promotion

Start a Kindle Countdown Deal or a Free Book Promotion. Note: Only KDP Select books are eligible. Only one promotion can be used per enrollment period.

◉ Kindle Countdown Deals
◯ Free Book Promotion

Create a Kindle Countdown Deal

Go for Free Book Promotion and set the free days about a week from now - Monday to Friday. This will give us a decent lead time to complete the rest of the steps.

Now we want to get some **good reviews** on the book before launch. Your book should be currently set at $0.99 as per the last Part. Gets some friends and family to purchase the book and leave reviews.

Because the book is currently $0.99 I recommend giving a $1 to 20 or so people to go grab your book and write a review. You don't have to specify a good review but if they are friends and family hopefully they'll give you good reviews anyway!

Optionally at this point you can also submit your book to **free book giveaway sites**. There are lots of directories of these online - https://kindlepreneur.com/list-sites-promote-free-amazon-books/ is one example that has a list of them.

These sites will send your free book promotion out to their email lists and social media to get you more downloads. Some of these submissions sites are free, some are paid.

I wouldn't worry about paying unless you find a very attractive deal. This step is optional and I'd recommend only the free submissions.

Finally, the day before launch we **increase the price**.
Take it from $0.99 to the price that your best competitors charge - ie. $4.99. Check the competitor pricing and use this as a guide.

What this does is increase the perceived value of the free giveaway - instead of being discounted from $0.99 to $0 we're going to discount from $4.99 to $0.

2. Launch Day

We now have 5 days to shift as many free copies as possible.

We want to give away lots of free copies. This will shoot us up the Kindle rankings and help us secure reviews.

How we get the word out depends on our existing marketing channels. Assuming you have an audience already I'd recommend:
- Emailing your list day 1 with the announcement
- Pushing social media days 1-4
- Emailing again day 4-5 with "last call" announcement

If you don't have an audience you can run paid social media ads or (trickier but powerful) try to get coverage from someone else in the space who likes your work.

One particularly strong method is to find a community who is interested in your topic and start providing value in this space weeks if not months before launch. Obviously this will slow down your launch but it'll increase the chance of success.

Join a community and start providing massive value. Don't shill your book. Just be helpful. As you approach launch mention you've written a book - ask for feedback. Again you're not selling it, just making people aware. At launch post to thank the community for helping you put the book together and telling them there are free copies to thank everyone for the assistance.

Finally, the free book giveaway sites mentioned above will be more valuable here if you don't have an owned audience.

We also want reviews. You'd think that giving away hundreds of copies of your book would lead to hundreds of reviews right? Wrong!

Normally when I give away books for every 100 or so copies I'll get a single review. People are busy - I get it.

So we need to (ethically!) bribe them a little bit. When doing your giveaway announcements sweeten the deal a bit. Prepare some sort of gift that you'll give to everyone who sends you a screenshot of their review.

Give them an email or social media account to send the screenshot to and when they hit you up ping them over the gift. Review compliance will go through the roof!

Doing all this combined with choosing a low competition category as discussed in previous Parts should see your book hit #1 in the respective free Kindle category.

As soon as it does: screenshot that!

Spread the news to your followers that the book is #1.

This sort of screenshot is fantastic social proof that your book is doing well. People will see that and want to jump on the bandwagon and get a free copy. Ride that momentum.

Didn't hit #1?

The category was too competitive or your free giveaway didn't hit enough copies.

Not a problem - you now know the process and for next time can i) choose a more niche category and/or ii) prepare an audience beforehand.

I can't guarantee that you'll hit #1 but I can guarantee that by getting to this point you've learned a lot of skills and techniques that will make it much easier next time!

3. Post launch

As soon as your free period ends set the price back to $0.99.

We want to transition our momentum from the free Kindle charts to the paid charts so we drop the price.

Hold the lower price until you start ranking on paid. You want to be on the first page for your main keywords and ideally hitting #1-3 in one or more of your categories.

If/when this happens nudge price up to $2.99 so you can received the 70% royalty.

This only holds if your competitors are also around this price point - if everyone is playing at a lower price point you'll need to as well unless you have something very special.

Feel free to experiment with pricing at this time though - it can be easily switched in the KDP backend.

Once you are out of the initial launch I recommend also looking at some of the other marketing options available in the Dashboard.

The holy grail here are Amazon ads - if you can successful sell a book for less than the cost it takes to advertise it then you can really scale.

There are many other options in this dashboard that are free - A+ content for example is a great way to beef up the look and feel of your listing and "Nominate your book" is a nice bonus way to expand reach.

Take some time to learn about all the options and test them out with your book.

Recap

Well done. You're now a published author. Pretty cool huh?

Hopefully your book is making steady sales and bringing in an automatic income at this point. If it is: celebrate!

If it's not then you can use the built-in Amazon marketing methods or look to publishing your next book.

With AI the process is so quick that you can take multiple "at bats" without spending months or years writing and editing each one!

I'm currently publishing one book a week which is possible but not recommended unless you are a little bit mad!

You can also use your Kindle books alongside other business ventures and marketing. For instance I use Kindle books primarily to bring people to my newsletter and socials. Or as free giveaways connected to courses and other products.

Remember therefore that even if you don't currently have a #1 bestseller on your hands you do have a powerful business asset!

Playbook 4

Create an Online Course using AI

What is an Online Course?

With this business model you package up your expertise into a course which you sell to people who want to learn from you.

Structure of the guide

Over this playbook we're going to go into detail about:

Part 1: Course Topic Selection
Part 2: Course Structure
Part 3: Course Scripts
Part 4: Course recording and editing
Part 5: Course marketing

We're going to be focusing on Udemy in particular, but these lessons are more widely applicable to Coursera, Skillshare, Youtube or self-hosting your own course.

I'm focusing on Udemy because it has the largest learning base. We're going to be tapping into that existing audience of learners rather than building an audience from scratch.

Also, this is the platform I've personally had the most success on and so am therefore most qualified to talk about. Better than me making stuff up!

Here's one of my courses on Udemy which has 26,000+ students and 4.6 star average review on 458 ratings.

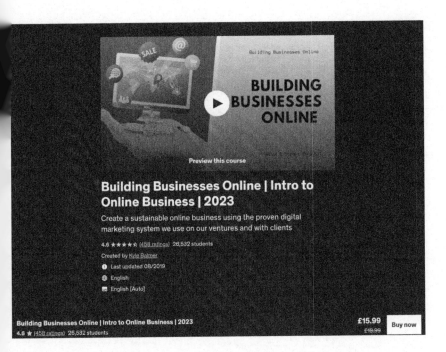

Once you've created your course though you can test it out on different platforms. Or publish it on multiple platforms - just make sure to check the T&Cs on each platform for exclusivity clauses.

Course Topic Selection

In this part we're going to focus in on what exactly your course is going to be about - the topic and your particular unique selling point.

1. Topic brainstorming

You could create a course about something you don't know anything about.

AI will allow you to do this.

However, the end result will be uninspired, dull and probably full of errors!

Instead we're using AI to help us with the process of creating a course - not to do all of the work for us! Therefore the course we are creating should be a topic that we have both knowledge and skills in.

You may already know what this is. If so great; skip to the next step. But if you are at a loss we'll use ChatGPT to help come up with ideas.

Let's start with a simple prompt to start thinking about topics.

Act as an online education specialist.

I am preparing an online course and want assistance with the course ideas.

My areas of expertise are in: [insert skills/ knowledge]

Generate 10 unique course ideas related to each area of expertise.

Please also suggest a key learning objective for each course..

Where the prompt says [Insert skills/knowledge] add as many of your areas of expertise as possible.

The more you add the more ideas ChatGPT will throw at you.

These can be professional expertise from your work or more personal skills and knowledge from hobbies and interests. Don't limit yourself at this point - we want to go wide and get the creative juice flowing.

Prompt Output

Here is an example output for "digital marketing" which is one of my areas of expertise.

Digital Marketing:

1. **Course Title:** "Search Engine Optimization (SEO) for Business Growth"
   * **Key Learning Objective:** Learn SEO techniques to increase website visibility, drive more organic traffic, and grow your business.
2. **Course Title:** "Data-Driven Marketing: Analytics for Strategy Development"
   * **Key Learning Objective:** Understand how to leverage data and analytics to inform marketing strategy, optimize campaigns, and improve return on investment.
3. **Course Title:** "Social Media Marketing: Building Brand Awareness and Engagement"
   * **Key Learning Objective:** Understand the strategies to use social media effectively for brand awareness, customer engagement, and lead generation.
4. **Course Title:** "Content Marketing: Driving Traffic and Building Authority"
   * **Key Learning Objective:** Learn how to create, distribute, and measure high-quality content that attracts and retains a clearly-defined audience.
5. **Course Title:** "Email Marketing: Strategies for Customer Retention"
   * **Key Learning Objective:** Understand how to design and implement successful email marketing campaigns for customer acquisition, retention, and loyalty.

Note the multiple topics here: SEO, data-driven marketing, social media marketing, content marketing, email marketing etc.

These are the sort of topic ideas we want to extract and use in the next step. So note down any that are of interest and we'll be finding out which are good course ideas to pursue.

2. Udemy Instructor Insights

Once you have a handful of potential course topics in hand we need to check how the market looks.

It's not enough to build a course that we are interested in. It also needs to be something that:

- Has lots of interested learners
- Has competition we can beat

For this we'll use Udemy's Marketplace Insights tool. You'll need an Instructor's account on Udemy to do this. This is free and quick to set up here. Go ahead and make an account.

Once you are in your instructor's account go to Tools > Marketplace Insight tool. You'll see a search bar like this:

Go ahead and type in one of the topics from step one. Chances are it's a topic on Udemy - if not try variations of the word and you'll find it. Udemy has a huge range of topics.

You'll be presented with a HUGE amount of information about the topic.

For the topic "ChatGPT" for instance I can see that demand and competition is high. Unsurprising considering the top teacher makes $65,000/month.

Student demand	Number of courses	Median monthly revenue	Top monthly revenue
high	high	$52	$65,920
		per month	per month

I can also see the top keywords people use to find the content as well as related topics:

Top search keywords		Other topics of interest	
chatgpt	32%	Generative AI	
chat gpt	9%	AI Text Content Generation	
prompt engineering	8%	Productivity Apps	★
ai	5%	Prompt Engineering	
midjourney	2%	Midjourney	
chatgpt prompt engineering	1%	AI Art Generation	
gpt	1%	Artificial Intelligence	
generative ai	1%	DALL·E	
chatgpt masterclass	1%	Microsoft Power Platform	★
chatgpt 4	1%		
Show less			

Make sure to investigate those other topics if they are relevant to your skills. Especially those with stars - those have high demand and low competition.

Further down the page you'll also be shown the top courses in the topic, their number of sales and their average review ranking.

Lots and lots of valuable market information that we"ll be using to decide our topic.

Right now go through your topic list from step 1 and look for high demand topics that (ideally) have low or medium competition. These will be the sweet spot.

Collect up a few of these as your shortlist. Feel free to choose a topic now or continue to the next step with a few options if you are still uncertain.

3. Competitive analysis

Once you have one, or a small handful, of topics we want to do some competitive analysis.

This process takes some time so ideally do it with less than 5 topics.

In Udemy's Marketplace Insight tool scroll down to the Top Earning Courses section. You should see 5 courses here. These are the most successful and the ones we want to emulate.

Open up new tabs/windows for each course.

Act as a course creation strategist.

I will provide you with the details of 5 courses around [topic]

Review each of these courses and output in a table a competitive analysis

The columns are:

- *number of students*
- *- number of reviews and star rating*
- *- length of course in hours*
- *- relative strengths of course*
- *- relative weaknesses of course -*
- *unique content in this course not available in other courses*

- I will provide 5 courses worth of details. Please prompt me for each course one at a time until you have all five and then perform the analysis.

For each course copy/paste the:

- What you learn
- This course includes
- Description

The description text may be too long for ChatGPT to process. If so take the first few paragraphs as they should be the most important.

Prompt Output

Make sure to add in the [topic] in the prompt and hit enter.

ChatGPT will then ask for details for each of the 5 courses.

If you provide information but ChatGPT is still missing info it will prompt you for more.

Keep going until you've added information about all 5 courses. Then ChatGPT will begin its analysis. It may need to be told to begin the analysis after the 5th course- just say "start" or "ok" and it'll begin.

The output will look like this:

Course	No. of Students	No. of Reviews & Star Rating	Length (Hours) & No. of Lectures	Relative Strengths	Relative Weaknesses	Unique Content
Course 1: ChatGPT Complete Guide	75,044	9,388 reviews, 4.6 rating	14 hours, lectures not specified	Comprehensive coverage of AI tools; Hands-on exercises	Could be overwhelming for beginners; Some parts might need programming knowledge	Multimodal use of AI tools; DALL-E 2
Course 2: The Complete Guide to ChatGPT & OpenAI APIs	21,031	1,836 reviews, 4.7 rating	12 hours, lectures not specified	Focus on ChatGPT and OpenAI APIs; High rating	Might be a bit advanced for beginners; Less hours compared to others	Integration of OpenAI's APIs into custom code; AutoGPT and LangChain
Course 3: ChatGPT Guide for Beginners to Experts!	44,118	6,222 reviews, 4.5 rating	9 hours, lectures not specified	Wide array of applications covered; Pro-tips on usage	Might not delve deep into certain topics due to breadth of topics	Use of ChatGPT for SEO, E-commerce, translation; Academic use of ChatGPT
Course 4: Build Solutions and Apps with ChatGPT	20,988	2,179 reviews, 4.5 rating	6.5 hours, lectures not specified	Focus on creating applications and integrations	Fewer hours; Could use more theoretical backing	App creation with business platforms and no-code development apps
Course 5: Unleash ChatGPT and GPT4	11,394	859 reviews, 4.8 rating	13 hours, lectures not specified	Detailed content on GPT-4; High rating	Assumes familiarity with Python APIs; Fewer students could indicate niche content	Use of GPT-4; Text embeddings Use of Whisper for audio file translation

This gives us a comparative analysis of the top 5 Udemy courses in our niche.

Because these are the top 5 they are doing something right - we want to learn from them. So this is invaluable information. In the next step we'll go a little further with this competitive intelligence.

4. USP/ Gaps in the market

In the same prompt window go ahead and add this prompt below the comparative table.
If you have navigated away from the previous chat look in your chat history to find the comparative analysis again.

Now use this prompt:

> *Based on the comparative analysis you just completed, propose a course that takes the best from each, and avoids the weaknesses.*

No additional info needed - ChatGPT will take all the information it needs from the comparative table above.

Prompt Output

 Absolutely, based on the comparative analysis and understanding the unique strengths and weaknesses of each course, we can propose a course that takes the best from each, and avoids the weaknesses. Here is a proposed course:

Course Title: "AI Revolution: Mastering ChatGPT, GPT-4 and OpenAI APIs with Practical Applications"

Course Highlights:

1. **Comprehensive Coverage:** The course would provide a complete understanding of AI tools, including ChatGPT, GPT-4, OpenAI APIs, DALL-E, and more, ensuring that students get a broad and deep understanding of the AI landscape.
2. **Practical Implementations and Applications:** Drawing inspiration from Courses 3 and 4, we will focus on practical applications of these tools in real-world scenarios including SEO, E-commerce, translations, creating apps, and integrations with business platforms.
3. **Guided Prompt Engineering:** A major focus will be on teaching students to engineer perfect prompts and fine-tune the models' performances, which was a strength in Courses 1 and 2.
4. **Advanced Concepts Simplified:** Our course will cover advanced topics like text embeddings and whisper for audio files, similar to Course 5, but will make sure to present them in a simplified way that can be understood even by beginners.
5. **Hands-on Approach:** Like Course 1, this course will also focus on hands-on learning, with many exercises and practical projects that allow students to apply what they've learned.
6. **Beyond Theories - Real-world tools:** We will provide tutorials on how to integrate these tools into no-code platforms and popular business platforms. This feature, inspired by Course 4, will empower students to apply their knowledge in real-world settings.
7. **Pro-tips and Tricks:** Inspired by Course 3, we will provide pro-tips and tricks on usage, which would come from experienced industry professionals.
8. **All-levels Welcome:** This course will be designed in a way to cater to both beginners and advanced students. The content will be broken down into digestible sections with clear learning paths for different student profiles.
9. **Community and Continued Learning:** Students will have access to a community forum for course-related discussions and doubt resolution. Regular updates and additional resources will be provided for continued learning beyond the course.

By combining the best elements of each course and addressing the weaknesses, we aim to create an industry-leading course that is comprehensive, practical, accessible, and keeps students engaged and empowered.

This prompt takes all of the competitor information you provided, all the strengths and weaknesses, and suggests a course that is *better* than the others.

We will use this list of highlights later when we come to structure the course. So make sure to keep a copy.

5. Course title

Next we want a handful of potential titles for our course.

Use this prompt:

> *Provide me 10 more potential titles.*
>
> *Try to include keywords from this list, ordered from most to least important: [keywords]*

For the keywords refer back tot the Udemy Marketplace Insights tool and the top search keywords.

Top search keywords

chatgpt	32%
chat gpt	9%
prompt engineering	8%
ai	5%
midjourney	2%
chatgpt prompt engineering	1%
gpt	1%
generative ai	1%
chatgpt masterclass	1%
chatgpt 4	1%

Prompt Output

 Sure, based on the keywords you've provided, here are 10 potential course titles:

1. "ChatGPT Masterclass: Unleashing the Power of Generative AI through Prompt Engineering"
2. "Beyond AI: Advanced Prompt Engineering with ChatGPT and Midjourney"
3. "The Ultimate Guide to ChatGPT: Master Prompt Engineering & Midjourney in AI"
4. "Demystifying AI: A Comprehensive Guide to ChatGPT, Midjourney, and Prompt Engineering"
5. "Transformative AI: Understanding ChatGPT and Generative AI through Prompt Engineering"
6. "ChatGPT & Midjourney: The Future of Generative AI and Prompt Engineering"
7. "Navigating the AI Landscape: Prompt Engineering with ChatGPT and Midjourney"
8. "Prompt Engineering Mastery: Unleash the Full Potential of ChatGPT and Generative AI"
9. "Exploring AI Frontiers: From ChatGPT to Midjourney, Prompt Engineering and Beyond"
10. "AI, ChatGPT & More: A Practical Guide to Prompt Engineering and Midjourney"

These titles aim to capture the depth and breadth of your course while highlighting the key themes you've identified.

Choose one that includes the keywords but also *sounds* good. You'll be better than ChatGPT at choosing this.

Pulling it together

Phew!

In this part we started with idea generation, worked through market and competitive research and came out the other side with a set of guidelines for the "perfect" course as well as a name to go along with it.

That's a lot of work done. In fact, the most important work.

We're going to build on these elements, especially the set of guidelines for the perfect course, in the next Part as we start to structure and write the course.

Course Structure and Planning

In this part we're going to be focusing on structuring and planning our online course.

This is a big and complex task but I've written an equally big and complex prompt to do the heavy lifting for you.

1. Length of course

Before we beginning structuring everything we need to know the length of the final course.

First question: do you want to make the course free?

Why would you want to make it free?

If you have other products/services or simply want to build up an audience then you can use a free course on Udemy to get to a lot of people. Then you take them from the course over to your social media and email list and sell them your other products and services.

Making the course free gets it into the hands of the most amount of people - thus driving your other business further down the line.

If you want to do this then the course has to be under 2 hours. That's the limit for free courses on Udemy. So your course length should be 2 hours.

Don't want the course to be free? No problem - here are the next considerations.

If you want the course itself to be the income generator then you can have any length of course.

If this is the case look at the length of the top selling courses in your Topic and replicate this.

In AI for instance they are all around 15 hours so for a paid course I'd go for around 15 hours.

A caveat to this : if your competitive analysis and perfect course guidelines (from Part 1) came up with suggestions to make your course longer or shorter then follow these suggestions.

The final thing to keep in mind is your time. A longer course will take longer to make- obviously! If this is your first course think about keeping it shorter at a couple of hours rather than a marathon 20 hours course!

In any case, for this step come up with a final number for how long you want the course to be. We'll be using this to help structure the course.

2. Structure prompt

Using all of our work so far we can now plug into this chunky course structure prompt. I'll work through it piece by piece after so you understand what's going on here.

Use this prompt in your existing chat that contains data on the 5 competitor courses you analysed.

Why? Your perfect course guidelines will likely refer to the 5 competitors so use the same chat so that ChatGPT has sufficient context:

> *Act as an online course expert*
>
> *I'm preparing a course about [topic]. You will decide the Sections and Lessons this course will contain and build a course structure.*
>
> *The course title is [title]*
>
> *The total length of the course should be [total length]*
>
> *The course structure should be split into Sections, each section containing multiple Lessons. Adjust as necessary to fulfill the total course length. Each section should end in a Quiz.*
>
> *Each lesson should be no more than 10 minutes. There should be 5-8 minimum lessons per section. Split the sections into*

multiple lessons accordingly, making sure to hit the total course length.

Make sure that the total course length adds up to the total length provided above.

The course structure should follow these guidelines

#begin perfect course guidelines#
[paste perfect course guidelines]
#end perfect course guidelines#

Provide me with a course structure in tabular format containing:

Section, Lesson title, Brief description, Lesson learning outcome, length of lesson in minutes, total cumulative course length

Plug in your Title, Topic, Total Length and the guidelines created in Part 1 about creating a perfect course.

Prompt Output

ChatGPT will create a table of your course's structure. This will be very long - so here's just a sample of the top of my table:

Section	Lesson Title	Brief Description	Lesson Learning Outcome	Length of Lesson (Min)	Cumulative Course Length (Min)
1	Introduction to AI and ChatGPT	Understand the fundamentals of AI and ChatGPT	10	10	
	Understanding Generative AI	Dive into the concept of Generative AI	Grasp the concept of Generative AI	10	20
	Overview of OpenAI	Introduction to OpenAI and its mission	Understand the vision and mission of OpenAI	10	30
	Quiz 1	-	-	10	40
2	Introduction to GPT-4	Deep dive into GPT-4 and its capabilities	Understand GPT-4	10	50
	GPT-4 in Action	Showcase of GPT-4 in real world scenarios	Understand the application of GPT-4	10	60
	Comparing GPT-4 and ChatGPT	Understanding the similarities and differences between GPT-4 and ChatGPT	Identify the pros and cons of GPT-4 and ChatGPT	10	70

3. Manual edit

Remember in the last Part where I suggested choosing a topic you are familiar with and have skill in? Here's why.

Now you need to go through the structure you've been provided and give feedback to ChatGPT

For example in the image above I see a lesson called "Comparing GPT-4 and ChatGPT".

That's not a helpful lesson - GPT-4 is a version of ChatGPT which means this comparison isn't a helpful one. I'd want to drop this lesson.

Go through your course structure and note the lessons you want to delete. For these tell ChatGPT to drop or delete these lessons.

For other sections and lessons you might want to reorder the content. Again, just type this into ChatGPT ("reverse the order of lesson x and lesson y").

For some you may think ChatGPT hasn't added enough detail or has too much detail. Ask it to add or subtract extra lessons until it's a bit more balanced.

This editing process is crucial to make your course valuable and needs to be done by you, a human expert. Thankfully editing a course outline is much easier than creating it from scratch.

4. Flesh out details

Once you've got your basic structure in a place you are happy with we're going to flesh out the details of each lesson.

We don't want to do this before the editing as we'll just end up with lots more information we need to get rid of later.

Use this nice simple prompt after your existing structure:

> *For each lesson add 3 main content bullet points.*
>
> *Add these into the existing table.*

Prompt Output

Here's a snippet:

3	Basics of Prompt Engineering	What is prompt engineering?, Importance of prompt engineering, Strategies for designing prompts
	Designing Simple Prompts	Anatomy of a simple prompt, Best practices, Hands-on exercise
	Working with Complex Prompts	What makes a prompt complex?, Strategies for handling complexity, Hands-on exercise

This is a nice simple prompt that will give you more detail on each of the lessons that ChatGPT has added into the structure.

Again, go through and manually tweak, asking ChatGPT to add/delete or edit as required.

The more we do now with our structure the better our results in the next part where we start to generate content.

Pulling it together

This part has been big but hopefully the one large prompt I've provided will do a lot of the heavy lifting.

You still had to edit based on your own knowledge but doing so is easier than working from a blank page.

And rest assured that any editing work you've just done will pay back dividends in the next Part when we start to generate content. The more specific and focused your structure the more unique and engaging our final course content.

Speaking of - that's the next topic! For that, I'll see you on the next page!

Course Scripts

In this part we're going to be focusing on fleshing out our course outline and generating the scripts.

Initially I did build you a GIANT prompt that would automatically plough through your structure and pump out individual lesson script.

It was a thing of beauty. So complex. So complete. It would have made this process *real* fast and hands-off.

The problem: the scripts it made were rubbish! ChatGPT made perfectly *fine* scripts but they were not interesting or engaging enough for the limelight.

Instead I've come up with a workflow that takes a little longer (sorry!) but outputs far higher quality course scripts.

1. Rough draft

First we're going to generate a rough first pass of a script. We're going to do this one at a time because the following steps will make your final script far superior to batch production.

Here's the prompt:

> *Act as an online course expert*
>
> *Create a video script for [lesson] title*
>
> *The lesson should be [x] minutes long*
>
> *Using the information from above*
>
> *Provide image/video suggestions*
>
> *Provide timecodes*

Use this below the rest of your work from Part 2 so that ChatGPT knows the full lesson details. If you've lost those details copy paste them into a new chat then use this prompt.

I've suggest adding in the length of the video manually because ChatGPT was extremely inconsistent here. Adding it manually overrides any inconsistency.

Otherwise, simply plug in the title and ChatGPT will do the rest.

Prompt Output

Scene 1 *(00:00 - 00:10)*

[Video starts with upbeat music, a title card appears "Showcase of GPT-4 in Real World Scenarios"]

Narrator (Voice-over): "Welcome to today's lesson where we will be showcasing the power of GPT-4 in real world scenarios."

Scene 2 *(00:10 - 00:40)*

[Show visuals of AI applications in various industries]

Narrator (Voice-over): "The AI revolution is upon us. Its influence spans across industries, from healthcare to finance, and today, we will witness how GPT-4 is contributing to this revolution."

Scene 3 *(00:40 - 01:30)*

[Show visuals of content creation with AI: blogs, scripts, articles]

Narrator (Voice-over): "First up, let's talk about content creation. GPT-4 can generate human-like text, making it a powerful tool for creating blogs, scripts, and even books. Let's look at some examples."

2. Manual edits

ChatGPT will give us a basic draft of a script, hitting the learning outcomes and main points that we set up in the structure in Part 2.

If you just used this script the end result of the course would be...underwhelming.

It would feel like a course written by ChatGPT. And we don't want that!

Instead we'll use the first draft that has been generated and tell ChatGPT to make adjustments. Use your knowledge of the subject here.

For instance I got a lesson that including topics that I think are too detailed:

Scene 3 *(00:40 - 01:20)*
[Show screen recording of OpenAI API documentation]

Narrator (Voice-over): "Before we start, make sure you have access to OpenAI's API. If you haven't, follow the instructions on their documentation page to get started."

Scene 4 *(01:20 - 02:30)*
[Show code editor with Python script]

Narrator (Voice-over): "Let's start with writing a Python script. First, import the necessary libraries. We'll be using OpenAI's Python library for this project."

[Narrator explains the code]

API and Python would be too complex for the course I am designing. Therefore I'd simply tell ChatGPT this.

In this case I'd add a new prompt saying "API and Python are too complex for this course. Rewrite this lesson without reference to these topics".

ChatGPT would then rewrite, hitting the same learning objectives and main points but without mentions of APIs and coding languages like Python.

This is just an example - you'll need to read through and make similar suggestions directly to ChatGPT based on your knowledge of the subject matter.

Do this as your first pass of the script before moving onto the next steps where we refine the lessons.

3. Metaphors

The first refinement we want to add is the use of metaphors.

When you have the basic content of the script in place via manual editing - and not before! - we want to ask ChatGPT to come up with a nice metaphor to encapsulate the meaning of the lesson.

This is a teaching technique that will make the content easier to consume. You don't need to use this on all lessons but definitely try it on the more complex or abstract lessons you create.

Use this prompt:

> *Encapsulate the main point of this lesson in a metaphor that will aid the learner's comprehension and retention*
>
> *add this metaphor into the script and give me an updated version of the script.*

In the following output this was the initial version:

Scene 1 *(00:00 - 00:10)*

[Video starts with upbeat music, a title card appears "Showcase of GPT-4 in Real World Scenarios"]

Narrator (Voice-over): "Welcome to today's lesson where we will be showcasing the power of GPT-4 in real world scenarios."

Scene 2 *(00:10 - 00:40)*

[Show visuals of AI applications in various industries]

Narrator (Voice-over): "The AI revolution is upon us. Its influence spans across industries, from healthcare to finance, and today, we will witness how GPT-4 is contributing to this revolution."

Prompt Output

Which leads to this version with metaphor added:

Scene 1 *(00:00 - 00:20)*

[Video starts with upbeat music, a title card appears "Showcase of GPT-4 in Real World Scenarios"]

Narrator (Voice-over): "Welcome to today's lesson. Let's imagine GPT-4 as a master key. Just as a master key unlocks numerous doors, GPT-4 opens a myriad of possibilities in different scenarios."

Scene 2 *(00:20 - 00:50)*

[Show visuals of AI applications in various industries]

Narrator (Voice-over): "The AI revolution is upon us. And today, using our master key - GPT-4, we will unlock the doors to various real-world applications."

Don't like the metaphor ChatGPT uses? Ask for another.

Or, ask for a specific type of metaphor.

You can have some fun with this - here for instance is a nautical metaphor:

Scene 1 *(00:00 - 00:20)*
[Video starts with upbeat music, a title card appears "Showcase of GPT-4 in Real World Scenarios"]
Narrator (Voice-over): "Welcome aboard our voyage of discovery! Today, we're sailing the expansive ocean of AI with our ship, GPT-4, set to explore various islands of opportunity."

Scene 2 *(00:20 - 00:50)*
[Show visuals of AI applications in various industries]
Narrator (Voice-over): "In the vast sea of the AI revolution, our ship, GPT-4, enables us to navigate through a myriad of real-world applications."

Scene 3 *(00:50 - 01:40)*
[Show visuals of content creation with AI: blogs, scripts, articles]
Narrator (Voice-over): "Our first island is the Land of Content Creation. Here, GPT-4 proves to be a capable wordsmith, crafting human-like text for blogs, scripts, and even books."

4. Frameworks/Acronyms

Another way we can increase engagement and retention of our material is by putting information into frameworks with easy to remember acronyms.

What do I mean by this?

One of the most famous example is SMART goals. This is a framework for goal setting where goals are:

- **S**pecific.
- **M**easurable.
- **A**chievable.
- **R**elevant.
- **T**ime-bound

ChatGPT is really good at coming up with frameworks once it has your information.

I've got one for ChatGPT prompt engineering that I use in my material: RISEN.

- **Role:** The role or entity you want the AI to simulate.
- **Instruction:** Commands or instructions given to the AI.
- **Steps:** Sequence the AI should follow if applicable.
- **End goal:** The desired result from the AI's response.
- **Narrowing:** Constraints such as length, tone, etc. within which the AI should operate.

Whilst I had the basics of this framework in my head it was ChatGPT that helped me come up with the acronym that makes it much easier for students to learn.

Act as an education specialist

Analyse the lesson in the script and construct a framework into which to put the information

Apply single letters to each piece of the framework so that an acronym is formed. The acronym must be a word.

I'm going to apply this to a lesson on Pro Tips for Using ChatGPT.

Prompt Output

 The framework that can be created to encapsulate the information in the lesson is as follows:

1. **U**nderstanding: The basic knowledge of what prompt engineering is and how it is used in AI.
2. **S**trategy: The strategies and techniques employed in prompt engineering, such as the RISEN framework and being specific with prompts.
3. **E**xamples: Illustrative examples of how these strategies can be effectively employed.
4. **R**eiteration: The practice of trial and error to improve results.

These key aspects of the lesson can be remembered using the acronym **USER**, where U stands for Understanding, S for Strategy, E for Examples, and R for Reiteration. This acronym represents the learner as the 'user' of AI, fitting for the context of the lesson.

This is nice little acronym as it's also about users, who are the people "using" ChatGPT! That works nicely.

Even more powerfully you can ask ChatGPT to come up with more variations. One such variation would be **FACE**, where F stands for Fundamentals, A for Approach, C for Cases, and E for Experimentation.

Alternatively if you like most of the acronym but one letter doesn't work for you just ask for an alternative for that letter. The rest will be kept the same.

Including these sort of frameworks (and acronyms) is most powerful in lessons where there is a sequence of instructions you want the learner to be able to remember.

These sort of frameworks are also great because they'll be your intellectual property (IP) - they are unique ways of presenting information that you can use in your courses, eBooks, blog, newsletter and social media. They are extremely powerful IP assets.

5. Compiling your scripts

Once you are happy with the script for your first lesson we need to copy/paste it somewhere safe.

I personally use Notion. It's free and an excellent place to organise information for projects like this.

Here for example is my Notion for a (work-in-progress!) course on using ChatGPT:

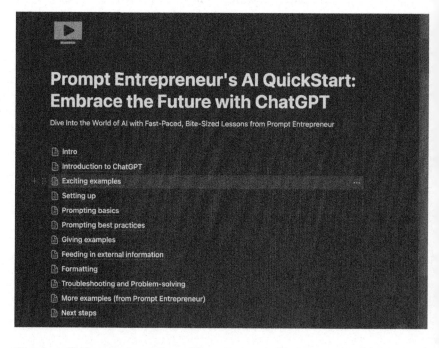

Each of those entries like Intro, Setting Up etc. are sections of my course

Each section has separate lesson documents inside it:

Prompting best practices

P - Precise: Make your instructions clear and precise. Vague questions or prompts ma...

R - Relevant: Keep your prompts relevant to the topic at hand. The model doesn't rem...

I - Iterative: If you're not getting the response you desire, refine and iterate your prom...

M - Moderate: Moderation is key. Extremely lengthy or complex prompts may confuse...

E - Explicit: Ensure that the expected format of the response is explicitly indicated in t...

You can also just use Notes or a Google Doc but Notion allows you to have a hierarchy of Course > Sections > Individual Lessons.

Once you've decided where to keep your scripts simply copy/paste them out of ChatGPT, saving them into your note taking system of choice.

We'll need to come back to them in the next step when we create our videos and having them all organised neatly now will save huge amounts of time. You don't want to be searching for each lesson's script in ChatGPT!

Pulling it together

In this part we've looked at how we flesh out a script and get it to a place where we are happy with its quality. I've also added in tips on adding metaphor or building a learning framework into the lesson to really up its value.

Your job now is to run this process with each of the lessons in your course.

This may take a little time - depending on the length of your course.

Remember though the alternatives. Either:

- Writing everything from scratch. Very time consuming.
- Auto generating everything from ChatGPT. Poor quality.

Instead we are leveraging ChatGPT and our knowledge to find a happy medium of speed and quality.

Next up we're pushing on to the actual creation where we turn these scripts into videos.

Course recording and editing

In this part we're going to finally start to put together our videos for our online course.

We've done a lot of prep to get to this point to make sure that our content is actually good quality.

There's no point spending time producing videos of crappy content. Therefore we focused on nailing the *script first*.

I used to produce TV/Film and you definitely want to work out the kinks when it's pen and paper and not video files! Scripts are a lot easier to work with than video footage believe me!

Let's get started.

1. Choice of production tools

Video production is a HUGE topic.

So I've been struggling to break this down into my usual "here's exactly what to do" approach.

This is make even more true by the fact that I want to balance your time and money input. For some people using paid for tools to produce video will be an efficient use of money. Whereas for others using free tools and putting in more personal work will be the answer.

I've debated this! I really have.

Here's the deal. I'm going to run through the options now and give you one that I'm choosing to detail.

I'll give you reasons and also more resources to use other tools if you aren't happy. It's hard to please everyone here so I'm aiming for the majority!

Options
a) The first method is to record and edit manual.

I've done this before, notably on my _https://learnchinesecharacters.academy/_ videos as well as my early Udemy courses.

The basic steps are:

- make a slide deck from your script in Powerpoint or Keynote
- screen record yourself going through the slides on a webcam using a tool like Loom
- edit using a free editor like iMovie, adding in stock videos and imagery from free sources like Pexels (_https://www.pexels.com/_) and stocksnap.io.

This is entirely doable and uses free or low price tools.

The main cost is instead your time.

I've done this process a few times and creating a video course takes months.

b) Descript

Descript (_https://www.descript.com/_) is an amazing tool for recording and editing. It's a complete suite of tools that can replace all the free versions I mentioned above.

Basically, creating a course in Descript would be the more premium version of the manual approach above. It costs about $12 or $24 dollars a month for the version of Descript you would need.

It still requires lots of work but the tool itself makes each sub-process smoother. You can expect to turn out a course in a couple of weeks.

c) Pictory

Pictory (_https://pictory.ai/_) is a new kid on the block and uses AI to produce videos much faster than if you were manually putting them together.

You upload your script and it automatically picks out suitable videos and images, adds written subtitles and generates AI voice over.

It has a free trial to play with and costs $19-39/month for a premium account, depending on how much you need to export.

d) Synthesia

Synthesia (_https://www.synthesia.io/_) is the "big boy" in AI video generation. It produces high quality corporate style videos, including custom AI avatars who can present your course like a real human being.

The quality of Synthesia is extremely high. As is the price. There's no free trial and the paid account is ~$30/month for 10 credits. Each credit gets you 1 minute of video! So we're talking $3/minute.

Wowzers.

Which to use?

These are a few of the big options you have.
If you have zero cash to invest into this then the
choice is easy - you'll need to go with the manual
free route.

However, we're Prompt Entrepreneurs. We want to
use the best AI tools available to us to get the work
done efficiently.

**As such this Part of the guide will be focusing
on using Pictory**.

This will allow you to create your whole course in a
matter of days for ~$40, a sum of money that will
be quickly recouped once you launch your course.

2. Video first draft

First up head over to Pictory to sign up.

It has a free trial. Yay!

It also doesn't need a credit card. Double yay!

You can sign up at *https://pictory.ai/*

Once in you'll see this:

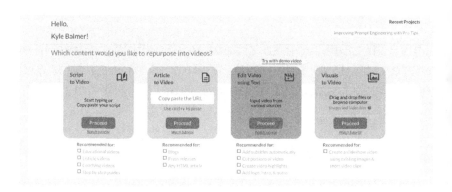

We want to go for **Script to Video**. Go ahead and click Proceed and you'll get the script editor.

Here it is with a script that I've copy pasted in.

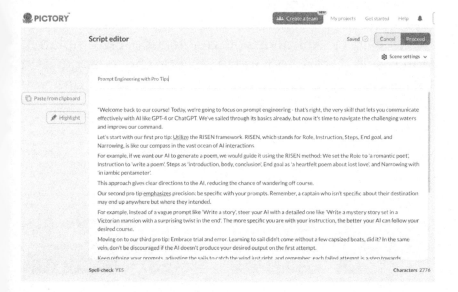

Notice that I've stripped the timecodes and description out of the script.

The scripts we have prepared, complete with image suggestions and time codes, are fleshed out enough to be used in any format. The extra detail will be invaluable in manual editing in particular. When using AI tools like Pictory though we'll just strip that info out quickly.

Go ahead and drop your script into ChatGPT and use the prompt:

> *Give me this script but remove timecodes and images suggestions*
>
> *Provide spoken script only*

Copy this stripped down version of the script into Pictory and hit Proceed.

Next, Pictory will give you a selection of templates. Don't sweat this too much as we can change it in the editor later. It's not final so just choose one you like the look of for now.

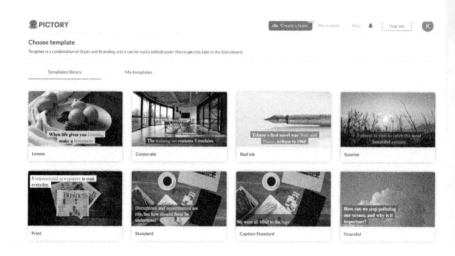

Pictory will now process the video. It doesn't take long - less than a minute. Once done it will spit out a first draft:

If you've ever manually prepared video content then chances are right now that your mind is blown.

Compared to manually preparing a similar video the speed Pictory works at is phenomenal.

Remember though: this is a first draft.

Like with all AI tools we're working with the tool. We aren't totally replacing ourselves.

3. Refining the video

The left sidebar in Pictory gives us access to the tools to refine our video. Take some time to explore the interface.

First we'll start by switching out images that don't make sense. Pictory will make a best guess about what videos and images to place in the video but sometimes it gets it wrong or the images are uninteresting.

Here's an example:

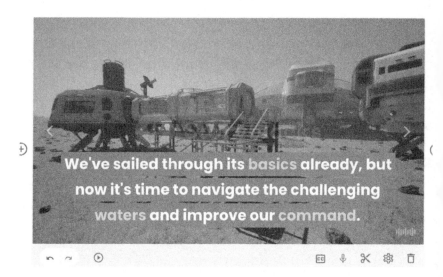

This part of the video is about moving from easy topics to more challenging topics. For some reason Pictory has chosen a video of a Martian space base. Let's switch that out.

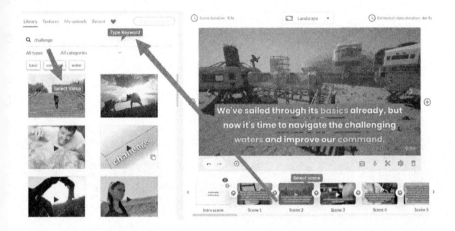

To switch this:

- Select the Scene at the bottom
- Type a keyword in the top left search bar within Library
- Select the video you want to use

This automatically switches the video and cuts the new video to length so it fits in the same Scene.

We've sailed through its basics already, but now it's time to navigate the challenging waters and improve our command.

Do this for each of the Scenes until you are happy with the overall results.

Next up, we want to add a voice over.

It's decision time now. You can either use one of Pictory's built in AI voices or record your own narration.

If you have a decent audio setup (a microphone or at least high quality headphones like Airpods) and you are comfortable recording you should.

AI voice-overs save a lot of time but aren't particularly engaging. They sound like AIs! The technology is improving all the time though.

Test out Pictory's built in AIs and see what you think. Also record some of your own narration so you can do a comparison.

Here's how to record narration:

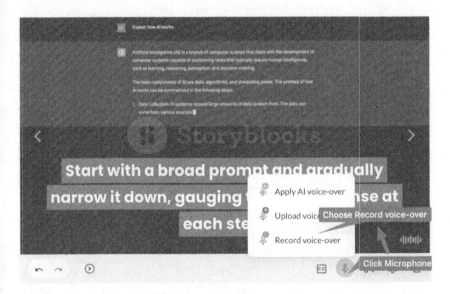

First click the microphone icon at the bottom of a selected Scene. Then choose Record Voice-over.
This will pop up a recording interface where you can record.

Importantly Pictory will match this up with the scene, saving you time trying to synch audio and video. Another massive time saver.

Speaking of sound, you probably have noticed that Pictory has chosen some **background music.**

If you don't want any music go to the Audio tab in the left sidebar then Background music. You'll see one music track has the word "Applied" next to it. To clear that music click the cross (x) to delete.

Alternatively you can replace the music with something more fitting. There are drop downs for selecting mood, purpose, genre and length. You can use these to filter the large music library and find something appropriate.

Generally it helps to have some music in the background and it fills empty space between narration. Just make sure that the volume isn't overpowering compared to the narration. Pictory does a good job of balancing thankfully.

Finally, some of you might be wanting to add your beautiful faces into the video. There's a nice simple way to do this. Just record the scene you want to replace using your camera, speaking the part of of the script in that scene. Then replace the visuals in that scene with the video and turn off any AI narration.

Once you've got the video customised hit the Preview button. That will show you the results of your work with all the changes applied.

Don't export just yet though!

4. Branding and export

Before you export your videos it's helpful to set up branding for your course. This branding will be applied across all your videos so it's helpful to set this up before you start exporting any videos.

Branding is set up in the left hand sidebar tab

Branding. Good name eh?

We specifically want an Intro and Outro.

Keep them extremely short, maybe 1 or 2 seconds tops. These should simply state the title of the lesson and have a quick animation.

For the Intro follow these steps:

First go to Branding in the left sidebar.

Then Enable Intro toggle on.

There may already be an intro template in place.
Delete the default and choose Import from Visuals.

This will take you to the video search we used
before to find visuals for our Scene.

Here's a clever tip: now just search "intro" and you'll get lots of nice background animations.

Once you've found one you like make sure to edit the Title (text is at the bottom) and upload your logo.

Do the same with the Outro but searching "outro" in the search. Or alternatively use the same animation as the intro.

Alternatively you can get intro and outro videos professionally made on Fiverr.com for a reasonable cost. This would be a good investment to increase the quality of your production very cost effectively.

Now go back to the Preview and check the results. Happy? Go ahead and export.

The free version will allow you to export a limited number of projects and they will all have water marks - so you will need a paid version eventually.

Just rest assured that you have saved thousands of dollars in hours by using an efficient tool like this.

Also, if you get all your videos processed in 30 days you only need to pay for one month. Not bad!

Pulling it together

Seems like a lot in this part.

But considering we covered a topic as complex as video creation this is pretty tight! This topic could have taken up the whole week if we were doing it the old way.

I for one am glad to not have to be making Powerpoint slide decks and screen recording everything in real time. Tools like Pictory make the process much faster - especially if it's your first time producing a course.

Instead of being a course creator and video producer you can focus on the course itself and let the technical parts be handled by tech.

Production will still take time, especially if you follow the Refinement steps outlined above. But course creation is now in hand and can begin.

We're moving into the back end of the process now. Next we look at packaging everything up, getting it published on Udemy and marketing.

Course Marketing

In the final Part of this guide we're going to finalise our course and set it up for success on Udemy.

Most of the marketing will be done by Udemy themselves once we have published the course.

However it's useful to get some early good reviews on your course to help it become more visible on Udemy. For this we'll do a little external marketing in addition to relying on Udemy.

1. Course Setup and Curriculum

We're going to let Udemy do the majority of the marketing for us.

Remember that this is why we chose to use Udemy rather than building a course on YouTube or a self hosted website.

This is because Udemy has a built in audience and will push your course for you.

But to make sure Udemy shows your course to its audience we need to ensure we've filled in as many details as possible about our course and optimised our course description.

First let's get our course online.

Log into the Udemy Instructor's interface. We created an Instructor's account back in Part 1 so refer to that if you don't yet have an account.

The majority of the set up process is simple: Udemy has a great course creation tool that walks you through everything you need to do.

First up hit New Course and start to fill in the basic details. You created a course title previously - go ahead and use that. For category just choose the one closest to your topic.

The main course creation interface looks like this :

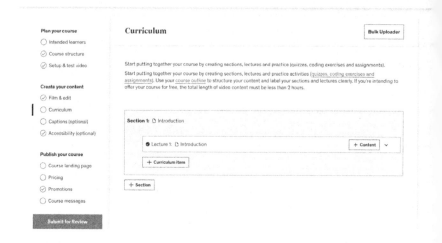

On the left you'll see the steps required.

You've already Planned your course and filmed everything so the first entry you'll be interested in will be **Curriculum** (shown in image).

In this interface you can import all of your content.

For simplicity I recommend

- Creating and naming all your sections as per your course structure
- Creating and naming all your lessons
- Bulk uploading all your videos using the bulk upload tool
- Assigning videos to each lesson
- Add descriptions for each lesson from the course structure

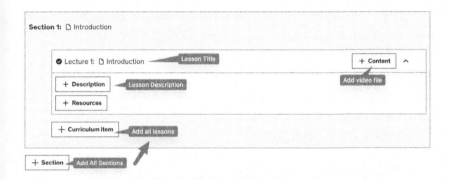

Refer back to the course structure we created in ChatGPT for all the text details you need. This includes the lesson description - just copy paste in the descriptions from the ChatGPT course structure table.

This process still takes some time but thankfully you have everything ready in a nicely formatted table.

Additionally if you titled your videos in Pictory your video file names will have the same lesson title. This makes assigning videos to lessons much faster.

2. Create Quizzes

This step is optional but adds a lot of value.

In Udemy you can add quizzes to reinforce student learning. This isn't required but it adds a lot of value to your course and increases engagement.

Crucially we also have a tool to help us make quizzes!

Udemy accepts multiple-choice quizzes. You can either make quizzes for every lesson or just one for each section - it's up to you.

To make a lesson quiz use this prompt

> *Act as a teacher.*
>
> *Analyse this lesson and give me 3 multiple choice questions that would reinforce student learning.*
>
> *Provide the question and 3 potential answers per question, 1 right, 2 wrong.*
>
> *Write a description of the quiz*
>
> *#copy/paste lesson script#*

Prompt Output

 Quiz Description:

This short quiz aims to reinforce your understanding of the concepts we discussed in the lesson 'Improving Prompt Engineering with Pro Tips'. The questions below will challenge your knowledge about the RISEN framework, the importance of precision in prompts, the trial and error approach, and the limitations of AI. Good luck!

Question 1: What does the acronym RISEN stand for in the context of prompt engineering?

A. Response, Instruction, Sequence, Example, Narrowing
B. Role, Instruction, Steps, End goal, Narrowing
C. Result, Input, Steps, Example, Numbers

Question 2: What was one of the key takeaways regarding the use of prompts in AI interactions?

A. Being vague and general in prompts often yields the best results.
B. It's best to avoid trial and error and get the perfect prompt at the first attempt.
C. Being specific and detailed in prompts improves the output.

Question 3: Which of the following statements is a limitation of GPT-4 or similar AI models?

A. AI models like GPT-4 can access real-time data and provide current, up-to-date information.
B. AI models like GPT-4 cannot produce human-like text.
C. AI models like GPT-4 cannot access real-time data or provide current, up-to-date information.

Correct Answers:
Question 1 - B,
Question 2 - C,
Question 3 - C.

Then simply copy paste these quiz outputs into the Udemy interface.

If you want to do one quiz per Section (instead of per lesson) then adapt the prompt so suggest one question per lesson and provide all the scripts below the prompt.

3. Landing Page

Next up is the landing page. This is the most impactful part of our Udemy marketing.

Our landing page text is where we performs SEO (search engine optimisation) to ensure we show up in Udemy.

We're going to pull in information from multiple places to write this text.

Here's the prompt:

Act as a SEO copywriter

Write a course description that will be on a landing page for my course on Udemy.

The goals are SEO visibility and an accurate description for potential customers.

Focus on these keywords : [udemy keywords]

Build upon this course basic description [description]

Include this course structure [course structure]

Include learning outcomes.

Use formatting including bold, italics, numbered lists and bullet points

Generate at least 2000 words of description.

It's a big prompt pulling from multiple sources. This ensures the output will be unique and tailored to your course.

Plug in details from previous parts. As much as possible.

You may find that ChatGPT can't handle all the information in one go - this will depend on how long your course and all its structure is.

If this is the case copy paste the prompt in and immediately hit enter. Don't fill in any missing details. ChatGPT will then ask you for the missing details.

This allows you to add details piece by piece so you won't hit limitations.

Prompt Output

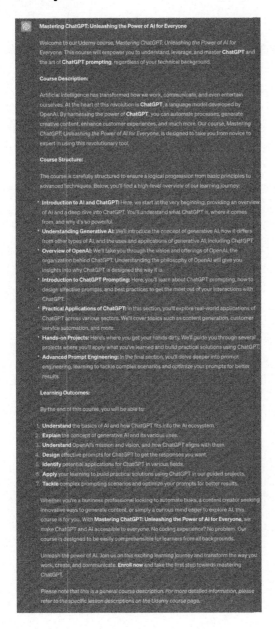

Mastering ChatGPT: Unleashing the Power of AI for Everyone

Welcome to our Udemy course, *Mastering ChatGPT: Unleashing the Power of AI for Everyone*. This course will empower you to understand, leverage, and master **ChatGPT** and the art of **ChatGPT prompting**, regardless of your technical background.

Course Description:

Artificial Intelligence has transformed how we work, communicate, and even entertain ourselves. At the heart of this revolution is **ChatGPT**, a language model developed by OpenAI. By harnessing the power of **ChatGPT**, you can automate processes, generate creative content, enhance customer experiences, and much more. Our course, *Mastering ChatGPT: Unleashing the Power of AI for Everyone*, is designed to take you from novice to expert in using this revolutionary tool.

Course Structure:

The course is carefully structured to ensure a logical progression from basic principles to advanced techniques. Below, you'll find a high-level overview of our learning journey:

* **Introduction to AI and ChatGPT:** Here, we start at the very beginning, providing an overview of AI and a deep dive into ChatGPT. You'll understand what ChatGPT is, where it comes from, and why it's so powerful.
* **Understanding Generative AI:** We'll introduce the concept of generative AI, how it differs from other types of AI, and the uses and applications of generative AI, including ChatGPT.
* **Overview of OpenAI:** We'll take you through the vision and offerings of OpenAI, the organization behind ChatGPT. Understanding the philosophy of OpenAI will give you insights into why ChatGPT is designed the way it is.
* **Introduction to ChatGPT Prompting:** Here, you'll learn about ChatGPT prompting, how to design effective prompts, and best practices to get the most out of your interactions with ChatGPT.
* **Practical Applications of ChatGPT:** In this section, you'll explore real-world applications of ChatGPT across various sectors. We'll cover topics such as content generation, customer service automation, and more.
* **Hands-on Projects:** Here's where you get your hands dirty. We'll guide you through several projects where you'll apply what you've learned and build practical solutions using ChatGPT.
* **Advanced Prompt Engineering:** In the final section, you'll delve deeper into prompt engineering, learning to tackle complex scenarios and optimize your prompts for better results.

Learning Outcomes:

By the end of this course, you will be able to:

1. **Understand** the basics of AI and how ChatGPT fits into the AI ecosystem.
2. **Explain** the concept of generative AI and its various uses.
3. **Understand** OpenAI's mission and vision, and how ChatGPT aligns with them.
4. **Design** effective prompts for ChatGPT to get the responses you want.
5. **Identify** potential applications for ChatGPT in various fields.
6. **Apply** your learning to build practical solutions using ChatGPT in our guided projects.
7. **Tackle** complex prompting scenarios and optimize your prompts for better results.

Whether you're a business professional looking to automate tasks, a content creator seeking innovative ways to generate content, or simply a curious mind eager to explore AI, this course is for you. With **Mastering ChatGPT: Unleashing the Power of AI for Everyone**, we make ChatGPT and AI accessible to everyone. No coding experience? No problem. Our course is designed to be easily comprehensible for learners from all backgrounds.

Unleash the power of AI. Join us on this exciting learning journey and transform the way you work, create, and communicate. **Enroll now** and take the first step towards mastering ChatGPT.

Please note that this is a general course description. For more detailed information, please refer to the specific lesson descriptions on the Udemy course page.

As always read the output and ask for changes as required.

This is the main element of your landing page covered - it's the course description that most determines search-ability.

For your course image I recommend Canva - just make sure to match Udemy's required image size.

Alternatively you can easily hire someone on Fiverr to do a course image for low cost.

4. Instructor Bio

Next is your instructor bio.

Writing about yourself can be hard so I've written up a script that will coach you through the process and generate a bio.

> *You are a brand manager who works with educators. You will help me write a bio about myself by guiding me through a set of questions.*
>
> *Ask these questions sequentially, not at the same time. Once you have collected an answer from me continue to the next question. Continue until all questions have been answered and then prepare the bio.*
>
> *The questions are:*
>
> *-name and main occupation ?*
> *-professional experience in the field you are teaching ?*
> *-personal hobbies and interests related to field you are teaching*
> *-what brought you to udemy to teach?*
> *-how will you best help your students?*
>
> *Once the questions have been answered you will prepare a professional yet approachable bio, written in the first person, intended to make people trust me and want to buy my courses.*

End with a gentle call to action to enrol in one of my courses

Once initiated ChatGPT will ask questions - just work through the questions and give as much information as possible.

At the end ChatGPT will generate a bio containing all the information.

Prompt Output

 Thank you for sharing, Kyle.

Now, let's create your bio.

Hello, I'm Kyle, a digital marketer with two decades of experience in the field. Along with holding an MBA, I have spent a significant portion of my career building online businesses, giving me a unique perspective on the challenges and opportunities you might face. My interests also extend into the realm of artificial intelligence (AI), and I'm passionate about exploring how these advanced technologies can transform the digital marketing landscape.

While I've run numerous in-person workshops and authored several books, I realized that I wanted to reach an even wider audience. That's why I've chosen Udemy as my platform to teach digital marketing. It gives me the opportunity to connect with learners from around the world, just like you.

My main aim as an educator is to ensure that all my students, regardless of their level of experience, feel confident and well-equipped in the field of digital marketing. This includes providing easy-to-understand AI lessons that you can practically apply in starting your own business.

If you're ready to start your journey in the world of digital marketing, or even if you're looking to expand your existing knowledge, you're in the right place. Join one of my courses today and let's explore the fascinating, ever-evolving world of digital marketing together.

Looking forward to seeing you in class!

5. Pricing

Choosing a price on Udemy can be tricky.

Here's the key though:

90%+ or Udemy sales are at a discount from the price you put - nearly nobody buys a course at full price. Instead Udemy constantly discounts courses.

This may seem annoying but it's the key to selling at volume!

It also means we set a high price, knowing it will be discounted.

For your price I recommend you first check competitors and their pricing bracket. Find courses that are a similar length to yours.

Now, take your price down 1-2 brackets from their price.

Why? Because you have zero reviews! They can sell for more because they have lots of happy customers and social proof - you don't yet.

So for now use their pricing as a guide and knock down 1-2 price brackets. Once you have a good amount of reviews you can increase the price.

6. Getting the word out

We chose Udemy specifically because they take care of most of the marketing.

However, it's useful to "prime the pump" and get some early positive reviews.

If you already have social media, blog, newsletter, podcast or other audiences great! You just need to make sure they know about your new course. I'm not going to worry about you guys too much as you already have a following!

If you don't have a following yet here are a couple of options.

First up, tell *me* about your course on Twitter. If you prepared it using this guide I want to help you out. I've got an audience and will use your course as a case study - that helps get the word out.

Second, tell family and friends. You can get your first handful of sales here easily. For launch set your price as low as possible (free if the course is under 2 hours) and give your friends and family members the cash to buy your course. They purchase, you reimburse. They leave a verified review. This is a nice simple way to get your first 10 or so 5 star reviews!

Third, do a community blitz. In preparation for your course launch (weeks before) find and start to participate in a community who will be interested in the course.

Where this community lives will depend entirely on your topic. Generally though there will be a community on Reddit, Twitter or LinkedIn Groups.

Begin participating, commenting, being helpful. Don't shill your course. Just become known and liked.

As you approach course launch mention that you have a course and want some feedback. Again, don't sell - genuinely seek feedback from the community.

As you approach launch maybe start to mention it's coming and offer some discount codes (Udemy allows you to do this).

Because you've only just joined this community you need to play this very cool - don't sell hard, don't spam. For the next launch make sure you have strong links or your own community!

Using one or a handful of these methods ought to get you the first handful of reviews which will help kickstart real sales.

Pulling it together

Well done for making it this far.

Recap

Boom!

We've covered a lot. This is a complex topic.

Creating a course is definitely a time investment but once it's up and running it's a great passive income earner.

From here you can also branch your course out onto Skillshare, Coursera and other platforms.

And importantly you are now building an audience of students. Do what you can (within platform rules) to move your students onto your social media accounts and your newsletter if you have one.

Doing this allows you to start multiplying your business in unexpected ways. You'll find you can sell your course students your ebooks, newsletter, coaching etc. once they are in your ecosystem.

And vice versa you can sell ebook readers, newsletter subscribers and coaching clients your courses!

Whilst building each pillar of your business takes time once a handful are operational you will begin to see exponential results.

And we can use ChatGPT and other AI tools like Pictory to radically accelerate our progress!
That's all for now Prompt Entrepreneurs.

Well Done

Most don't make it this far. Remember...

AI is moving fast. Extremely fast.

So I want you to do two things:

(1) **Follow me** on Twitter @iamkylebalmer:
https://twitter.com/iamkylebalmer

(2) **Subscribe** to my free email newsletter: Prompt
Entrepreneur: *https://
promptentrepreneur.beehiiv.com/subscribe*

Both options will keep you up-to-date and ahead of
the game when it comes to AI.

I'll see you there.

PS - Amazon will ask you to review this book. It
takes a serious amount of time to produce these
Playbooks. My only ask is you take a couple of
minutes to leave a review.

Useful Links

In this playbook I've shared various links. I've also in places used 'short links' to make it easier for you to type that URL. But sometimes these links 'break'.

Here's the full links for your reference:

My Twitter: *https://twitter.com/iamkylebalmer*

My Free Email Newsletter: *https://promptentrepreneur.beehiiv.com/* (or *https://tinyurl.com/3sp8unc4*)

AI Chat - ChatGPT: *https://openai.com/chatgpt*

AI Image creation - MidJourney: *https://www.midjourney.com/home/*

Email Software - Beehiiv: *https://www.beehiiv.com/?via=kyle-balmer* (or *https://tinyurl.com/53sszm6d*)

About the Author

Kyle Balmer is an established entrepreneur and renowned expert in leveraging AI for business growth. With decades of experience in launching and managing online businesses, Kyle has amassed a wealth of practical insights which he passionately shares with his audience.

He has successfully mentored over 26,000 students on Udemy, sharing his knowledge about entrepreneurship and the innovative use of AI in business. His approach to teaching focuses on the practical, guiding his students on their journey to starting and growing their own businesses.

As the author of the daily newsletter, "Prompt Entrepreneurs," Kyle provides his readers with in-depth insights into AI business models and actionable guides to generate new income streams, even for those with minimal technical skills. This daily roadmap to AI entrepreneurship has become a trusted source for many aspiring and seasoned entrepreneurs alike.

Stay connected with Kyle on Twitter (@iamkylebalmer) for real-time updates on AI developments in business and actionable tips on monetizing AI. Kyle Balmer is not just an author but a guide, helping you navigate the challenging yet exciting world of AI entrepreneurship.

Kyle studied History at Oxford University before setting off to Vietnam to set up the co-found the country's first private television station. After getting his MBA at NYU Stern in New York, Kyle moved to China to learn the "world's most difficult" language. Kyle now runs several online businesses, including those in the digital marketing, Chinese language, blockchain and AI spaces.

Other books in the series

For all upcoming AI and online business book releases be sure to subscribe to the Prompt Entrepreneur email :

"Uncover the secrets of talking to AI for online business success".

Look out for VOLUME 2 (Coming Soon).

Subscriber free to get notified first: *https:// promptentrepreneur.beehiiv.com/subscribe*

Printed in Great Britain
by Amazon

39787968R00205